Military Spending
and Industrial
Decline

Recent Titles in
Contributions in Economics and Economic History
Series Editor: Robert Sobel

The Strategic Petroleum Reserve: Planning, Implementation, and Analysis
David Leo Weimer

United States Oil Policy and Diplomacy: A Twentieth-Century Overview
Edward W. Chester

The Emergence of Giant Enterprise, 1860–1914: American Commercial Enterprise and Extractive Industries
David O. Whitten

The Marshall Plan Revisited: The European Recovery Program in Economic Perspective
Imanuel Wexler

The Rise and Decline of the American Cut Nail Industry: A Study of the Interrelationships of Technology, Business Organization, and Management Techniques
Amos J. Loveday, Jr.

The Dynamics of Development and Development Administration
Kempe Ronald Hope

Moving and Shaking American Medicine: The Structure of a Socioeconomic Transformation
Betty Leyerle

The Age of Giant Corporations: A Microeconomic History of American Business, 1914–1984; A Second Edition
Robert Sobel

The Anti-Monopoly Persuasion: Popular Resistance to the Rise of Big Business in the Midwest
Steven L. Piott

Working the Range: Essays on the History of Western Land Management and the Environment
John R. Wunder, ed.

Off the Track: The Decline of the Intercity Passenger Train in the United States
Donald M. Itzkoff

The Crash and Its Aftermath: A History of Securities Markets in the United States, 1929–1933
Barrie A. Wigmore

Synthetic Rubber: A Project That Had to Succeed
Vernon Herbert and Attilio Bisio

Military Spending and Industrial Decline
A STUDY OF THE AMERICAN MACHINE TOOL INDUSTRY

Anthony DiFilippo

CONTRIBUTIONS IN ECONOMICS AND ECONOMIC HISTORY,
NUMBER 68

GREENWOOD PRESS
New York • Westport, Connecticut • London

Library of Congress Cataloging-in-Publication Data

DiFilippo, Anthony, 1950–
  Military spending and industrial decline.

  (Contributions in economics and economic history,
ISSN 0084–9235 ; no. 68)
  Bibliography: p.
  Includes index.
  1. Machine-tool industry—Government policy—United
States. 2. Armaments—Economic aspects—United States.
3. Industry and state—United States—Case studies.
4. Technology and state—United States—Case studies.
I. Title. II. Series.
HD9703.U5D54 1986   338.4'7621902'0973   85–27144
ISBN 0–313–25179–7 (lib. bdg. : alk. paper)

Library of Congress Catalog Card Number: 85–27144
ISBN: 0–313–25179–7
ISSN: 0084–9235

First published in 1986

Greenwood Press, Inc.
88 Post Road West, Westport, Connecticut 06881

Printed in the United States of America

∞

The paper used in this book complies with the
Permanent Paper Standard issued by the National
Information Standards Organization (Z39.48–1984).

10 9 8 7 6 5 4 3 2 1

Copyright Acknowledgment
We gratefully acknowledge the **National Machine Tool Builder's Association**
for granting permission to reprint materials from *Economic Handbook of the
Machine Tool Industry*, 1978 and 1984 editions.

To Patty, Gemma, and Anthony and to my parents

Contents

Tables   ix

Charts   xi

Acknowledgments   xiii

1. An Introduction: Government Policy Contravenes the Machine Tool Industry   1

2. A Short History of Machine Tool Development and the Industry   13

3. The Industry: Its Structure and Problems   39

4. Machine Tool Demand and Defense Spending   89

5. The Politics of Survival   125

6. Perspectives on Position   157

Selected Bibliography   185

Index   193

Tables

1. Number of Machine Tool Establishments, 1958–1982   41

2. Concentration within the Machine Tool Industry, 1977   43

3. Geographic Location of Machine Tool Establishments by Divisions, 1958–1982   45

4. Net Income before Taxes as a Percentage of Sales for All Manufacturers and Machine Tool Companies, 1967–1983   45

5. Percentage Distribution of the Government R&D Expenditures of the U.S., West Germany, and Japan, 1963–1975   55

6. Age of Machine Tools in Seven Industrial Countries   64

7. Ratio of Backlogs to Total Shipments of Machine Tools, 1956–1983   68

8. Inventories of the U.S. Machine Tool Industry, 1958–1981   68

9. U.S. Imports of Complete Machine Tools from Selected Countries, 1965–1983   77

10. Imports as a Percentage of Domestic Machine Tool Consumption for the U.S., Japan, and West Germany for Selected Years, 1960–1983   77

11. Annual Percentage Changes in Real Domestic New Orders of Machine Tools and the Real Gross National Product (GNP), 1958–1983   90

12. The Top Six Industrial Consumers of Machine
    Tools   94

13. Prime Military Contract Awards for Machine
    Tools, Fiscal Years 1974–1983   94

14. Military Contracts as a Percentage of the Durable
    Goods Industry Sector of the GNP, 1951–1978   107

15. Estimated Annual Portion of Military-Induced
    Domestic Machine Tool Demand, 1970–1978   107

16. Share of the Eastern Bloc's Non-Communist Ma-
    chine Tool Imports Held by Six Major Capitalist
    Countries, 1962–1980   134

17. Manufacturing Workers' Hourly Compensation,
    Manufacturing Productivity, and Producer Prices,
    1960–1983   166

Charts

1. Gross Book Value of Depreciable Assets of the Machine Tool Industry, 1962–1981   49

2. Percentage of World Production for the U.S., Japan, and West Germany, 1964–1983   64

3. Total Employment in the U.S. Machine Tool Industry, 1958–1983   73

4. U.S. Exports and Imports of Machine Tools and Parts, 1958–1983   74

5. Share of World Exports, 1969–1983   78

6. Domestic New Orders of Machine Tools in Current and Constant (1967) Dollars, 1956–1983   92

7. Expenditures for Military Contracts and Domestic New Orders of Machine Tools, 1956–1978   100

8. U.S., West German, and Japanese Machine Tool Production, 1969–1983   116

9. Graphic/Conceptual Relation of R&D to Productivity Growth   170

Acknowledgments

This book has benefited from the valuable contributions of a number of people. Fred Block (Department of Sociology, University of Pennyslvania) read and commented on a few chapters of an earlier draft. Magali Sarfatti-Larson (Department of Sociology, Temple University) critically reviewed two earlier drafts of this work; her comments were very helpful, particularly in regard to style. Kyriakos Kontopoulos (Department of Sociology, Temple University) made many contributions to an earlier version of this book by helping me to formulate many of the central ideas and arguments found in this work.

Thanks is also due to Dr. John Houghton and Dr. Theodore Reed for their thoughtful suggestions and comments to Mrs. Dorothy Hagy, former secretary of the Department of Sociology at Lincoln University, who performed the tedious typing job and to Donna Del Rocini, secretary in the Department of Sociology at Lincoln University, who did some typing in the final stages of this book's production. Finally, I would like to express my gratitude to the National Machine Tool Builders' Association for making some information available to me.

Military Spending and Industrial Decline

An Introduction: Government Policy Contravenes the Machine Tool Industry

For more than three decades, the U.S. has advocated military spending as central to its national policy. But consistently high expenditures for defense have been disadvantageous to industry over the years. Indeed, as the chapters that follow this one will make evident, many of the problems the U.S. machine tool industry has had to contend with have resulted due to postwar military spending. Of utmost importance in this chapter, however, is to provide an explanation of how a permanent war economy has affected government action and how it has placed the American machine tool industry at a disadvantage relative to its major foreign competitors.

THE WAR ECONOMY AND ITS EFFECTS ON INDUSTRY

From 1950 to the present this nation has spent more than $3 trillion on defense. Through all of these years, the emphasis on military spending has varied, but essentially the fervid concern over national defense has remained salient. The emersion of supply-side economics in recent years, with emphasis being placed on sizeable and continuous increases in military spending, has taken attention away from Keynesian policy which was dominant throughout most of the postwar period.

As in the past, the manifest rationale for a growing military budget today has been the claimed purpose of national security. But more noticeably at the present time, the popular idea has become "security through strength." Beneath the rhetoric, however, the Keynesian stimulus resulting directly from defense expenditures is discernible. This was particularly true during the last recession when military spending continued to increase rapidly throughout the contraction.

An accompanying feature of the war economy in the U.S. from its outset has been the utilization of a large amount of the government's technological resources for defense purposes, something that has not occurred to the same extent in other advanced capitalist countries. Following the Second World War, along with the decline in defense expenditures, was the demobilization of the country's military research and development (R&D) apparatus. Primarily as a result of the Korean War and to a lesser extent due to the Soviet Union's success with the atomic bomb, the government began to remobilize the nation's R&D apparatus.[1] Together with its own organizations, the government relied on industry, universities and colleges, and other research centers to increase its technological competence in the area of defense. All told, from after the Korean War in 1953 up until 1965, the U.S. government spent over $80 billion for military and related R&D. In contrast, Japan and the Western European countries had been devoting much less of their total R&D efforts to defense and related technological expenditures. For example, in 1965 Japan spent a insignificant .014% of its gross domestic product on defense R&D; the corresponding figure for the U.S. was a noticeable 1.07%.[2] Very important also is the fact that by 1962, aided by lower labor costs, there were reportedly about 30 to 35% more scientists, engineers, and other technical personnel in eight Western European countries (England, France, West Germany, Italy, Belgium, Norway, Sweden, and the Netherlands) performing civilian work than in the U.S., where for some time personnel costs had been rising due in large part to abundant funding by the government for military and related R&D. And Japan in 1962, with only 50% the population of America, had an estimated 70% as many technical personnel as the U.S. doing civilian work.[3]

This difference in the technical direction of many foreign capitalist countries relative to the U.S. began to show up in the trade balance as businesses started to increase their importation of high-technology goods, along with other products. After a very healthy year in 1964, America's balance-of-trade surplus began to slowly but steadily deteriorate. Increased competition from abroad during the second half of the 1960s indeed had become a real threat to American economic hegemony. Though the U.S. had been experiencing balance-of-payments deficits for a number of years, to which military spending abroad by the state certainly made a contribution, by 1971, well before the oil crisis, the country's trade balance was negative for the first time in over seventy-five years. Moreover, by 1971 there was evidence indicating that in addition to slowing down the nation's economic growth, R&D expenditures for military and related purposes had reduced industrial productivity.[4]

There is very little doubt that a very significant decrease in defense spending by the mid–1960s would have created the conditions for the advancement of the country's technological know-how in the civilian sector. This is especially true since little transference generally has occurred from defense production to the civilian sector.[5] (However, for machine tool technology, transference appears to have been somewhat more than usual.) Increasing the nation's technological capabilities, apart from in the military sector, would have strengthened U.S. industries by improving their productivity, while also enabling them to compete more effectively with other advanced capitalist countries,[6] thereby forestalling the not-at-all-uncommon trade deficits of the 1970s. So due to the perpetuation of massive defense expenditures, the technological drain of funds and manpower evident in the 1960s continued into the 1970s,[7] and are even more apparent today.

Because the U.S. has spent excessively on military R&D and since nearly a third (at least) of the country's scientists and engineers have been supported by government money, primarily from the defense budget,[8] many of the problems in the civilian-industrial sector should be viewed as connected to these conditions. Two analysts have recently concluded that industrial development and military preparedness are not necessarily in agreement. What is more, the increasing specialization of military equipment could result in even fewer spillovers into the civilian sector while technical personnel are misused in defense production.[9]

There clearly is a major irony connected to the permanent war economy. Though large defense budgets were supposed to strengthen and revitalize the domestic economy, state planners during the fifties and sixties apparently did not have the prescience to comprehend the long-range harm that excessive and ongoing military spending would do to industries in the U.S. But for some time now the situation has been quite different. Despite the existence of trade deficits, productivity problems and the forceful arguments marking the contribution of the war economy to them,[10] the state still maintains a huge defense budget.

DEFENSE POLICY AND THE MACHINE TOOL INDUSTRY

The major point brought to the fore thus far has been that the maintenance of a war economy by government has been an impediment (and indeed an unanticipated one for some time) to the technical expansion and the industrial efficiency of the U.S. civilian sector. Exactly how continued military spending has affected the economics and the structural organization of the American machine tool industry will be the subject of major importance in subsequent chapters. But at this time what will be explicated is the impact of state action on the U.S. machine tool industry relative to the experiences of foreign metalworking builders with their governments. Such an explanation will enable the reader to place much of what is to follow after this chapter concerning the American machine tool industry and its foreign competitors—particularly builders in West Germany and Japan—during the post war years into a more comprehensive context.

An important feature of the permanent war economy is the military-industrial complex. The military-industrial complex is partially indicative of the kind of relationship that has developed between government and many corporations in the private sector in the U.S. since the Second World War. This relationship can perhaps best be described as harmonious, one in which the autonomy of the state is certainly much less than in other sectors of the polity. What is made clear from the term military-industrial complex is the interdependent relationship between the very immense military sector of the state and defense contractors, most especially the major ones. According to Seymour Melman's very inclusive definition:

Military-industrial complex means a loose, informally defined collection of firms producing military products, senior military officers, and members of the executive and legislative branches of the government—all of them limited by the market relations of the military products network and having a common ideology as to the importance of maintaining or enlarging the armed forces of the United States and their role in American politics. . . . The understanding, therefore, is that the main interest groups concerned tend to move together, each of them motivated by its own special concerns, but with enough common ground to produce a mutually reinforcing effect.[11]

Rather than a really autonomous military sector then, what has developed in the U.S. since the Second World War is a government defense apparatus that has worked more or less in tandem with many prime military contractors;[12] however, it is true that the state has been formally and primarily responsible for sustaining a war economy, somewhat analogous to its role when it was instituted over three decades ago. With the growth of prime military contract awards in the 1980s, this synergistic relationship between the state and procurement contractors is becoming more and more inviolable to external sociopolitical pressures.

While the military sector of the government and prime contractors, particularly the major ones, have experienced a more or less harmonious relationship in regard to military production, much less cooperation has existed between the business world and government in the civilian sector, due primarily to the state's preoccupation with building a formidable and technologically advanced defense apparatus. This is indicated by virtue of the fact that federal R&D expenditures have been overwhelmingly devoted to defense and related purposes. (For example, in 1975, 66% of all of the federal government's R&D funds went to defense and space projects.) As a result, a very cooperative relationship has existed between the Pentagon and a few industries, with the aerospace industry best exemplifying this relationship. On the one hand, this has led to the production of highly sophisticated missiles and aerospace vehicles. On the other hand, an industry, such as the machine tool industry, though indispensable to the production of defense equipment, yet while not centrally located within the military-industrial complex, has suffered from the policies of the government since it has been in desperate need of R&D funds in order to be competitive with foreign producers. A government bent on fulfilling military objectives, however, has been unable to advance the technological competence of industry, and specifically the machine tool industry, other than through the defense sector. In short, the very uncooperative relationship that has existed for the most part between the government and the U.S. machine tool industry in regard to technological assistance for civilian purposes has not been the least bit helpful in improving its international competitiveness, or its productivity.

An additional factor concerning the government's relationship with the U.S. machine tool industry and business in general has been the application of military-Keynesian policies through much of the postwar period. Though the war economy has been an ongoing phenomenon, an essential part of its usefulness had been that as an economic regulatory device the government had sporadically increased or decreased military expenditures for a considerable period of time.[13] (By the late 1970s the state abandoned the policy of periodically decreasing military expenditures.) While it is unknown to what extent other industries have been injured by military-Keynesianism, the utilization by the government of these policies (indicated by fluctuating defense expenditures) has been quite harmful to the domestic business of the machine tool industry. For now, it is sufficient to point out that such policies made the machine tool industry more sensitive to the business cycle, its biggest problem, and this in turn contributed to other problems such as a poor trade balance and reduced expenditures for R&D.

Two important structural characteristics stemming from the government's overreliance on defense have been earmarked above. Both the sporadic nature of military-Keynesianism, in the past, and the generally uncooperative relationship of the state with industry in regard to its technological development, apart from in the defense sector, have not been beneficial to the U.S. machine tool industry. In this decade it is the technological depletion resulting from rapidly growing military R&D funds and the failure of the government to develop an adequate and planned industrial policy for the civilian sector that will decrease the competitiveness of the machine tool industry. Therefore, despite the form it has taken—whether it be military-Keynesianism or a supply-side policy emphasizing continuous increases in military expenditures—to some extent defense production has been a counterproductive force at work on the private sector, and, for our immediate purposes, on the machine tool industry. Permanently being prepared for war unexpectedly has created problems for the U.S. machine tool industry. Because a war economy is in large part the antithesis of civilian production, efficiency, and technical competence, it becomes easier to comprehend how long-term defense spending in the U.S. has been a negative force operating on the U.S. machine tool industry, especially after considering the fact that its very aggressive foreign competitors have not really been burdened by military expenditures.

Foreign economies, like West Germany and Japan, having not been encumbered by permanently large war budgets and military-Keynesianism, have not experienced fluctuating defense expenditures of any significance. This means that these foreign machine tool builders have not had to worry about sporadic and defense-induced fluctuations in business originating in their respective state apparatuses and resulting from the use of military-Keynesian policies. Moreover, unlike in the U.S., a cooperative relationship between the state and foreign machine tool builders has existed for the common purpose of advancing metalworking technology. The importance of this type of cooperative relationship should not be underemphasized, for over time it has been instrumental in developing the West German and Japanese machine tool industries into the two biggest and fiercest competitors of American builders. As Chapter 3 will fully document, the technological edge once securely held by the U.S. machine tool industry has noticeably deteriorated as Japanese and West German producers have been benefiting from financial assistance from their governments—governments that have been concerned with strengthening their civilian industries.

This cooperative, technological relationship that has existed between foreign governments and machine tool builders abroad is indicated in what follows. Part of the public statement of the

National Tool Builders' Association before a Senate Subcommittee in March of 1978 includes a letter submitted by the association's president. This letter makes evident that the governments of a few foreign countries cooperate economically with industry in the area of R&D. In regard to Canada, France, and West Germany, the letter underscores the large amount of government support given to private industry for R&D in these countries, which, of course, includes the machine tool industry in each of these nations. Most interesting is the comment made concerning Japan. According to the president of the National Machine Tool Builders' Association, the government of Japan "takes a very paternalistic view of domestic industry, working closely with the private sector to develop and promote new exportable products through the Ministry of International Trade and Industry (MITI)."[14] In short, where defense spending has not become a major concern of the state, a technical-cooperative type of relationship has existed between government and machine tool builders. Had U.S. machine tool builders been exposed to the same technical-civilian alimentation made available to foreign producers by their governments, they would have been somewhat better equipped to meet the foreign competition. But such technical assistance could not have been made possible given the state's wholehearted efforts to continuously advance the nation's military capabilities.

An indication of the uncooperative relationship between the defense sector of the state and the civilian sphere in the U.S. is also evident in regard to the issue of government export restrictions to many of the communist countries. At least partly because it has been armed to protect its allies, to some extent the defense sector has interfered with the exportation of capital goods, including machine tools, from the country (and especially in recent years, more so than what has occurred in other advanced capitalist nations). Thus these formal export controls in the U.S. are related to the government's dominant military position within the Western world. From the perspective of many in the business world, and certainly from the view of the machine tool industry, this is a violation of a basic principle of free enterprise.

Nonetheless, it should be made clear that there is a tendency within the state apparatus, due in part to its large defense sector, to work against the short-term interests of the business world when it comes to export controls. The fact of the matter is that the defense sector, despite its definite intention to preserve the domestic and international status quo, cannot help but militate against the interests of civilian industry at times in the area of commercial exports. A conflict of interests arises because, while the primary concern of business is with unimpeded growth, the military part of the state apparatus has been responsible for protecting all "reasonable" governments. Similar to the way defense production and civilian production are opposites, the perennial quest for larger markets that is characteristic of business and which includes the desire for the elimination, or at least the minimization of all political export restraints, contravenes the protective role of the government in the U.S. So, somewhat problematic for the American machine tool industry has been the conflict between its desire for expanded markets and the interest of the state's defense sector in safeguarding much of the world.

CONCLUSION

Sustained and exhorbitant military spending throughout most of the postwar period has been detrimental to industry. Specifically, because of the government's very large military component, more harm than good has been done to the American machine tool industry. This industry's overall performance, including its technological competitiveness, has been distorted by a war economy, a situation much different for many foreign machine tool builders.

While the primary concern of this work is with examining the U.S. machine tool industry during the years following the Second World War, some understanding of the history of this industry is nonetheless appropriate. Having some historical background will enable us to draw out more clearly the impact of military spending on the machine tool industry in the postwar years. In the next chapter we will briefly survey the history of machine tool building and the industry up to the Korean War.

NOTES

1. Herbert J. York and G. Allen Greb, "Military Research and Development: A Postwar History," *Bulletin of the Atomic Scientists*, January 1977, p. 17.

2. See Organization for Economic Co-operation and Development, *Technical Change and Economic Policy* (Paris: OECD, 1980), p. 40.

3. See J. Herbert Hollomon and Alan Harger, "America's Technological Dilemma," *Technology Review*, July/August 1971, p. 38; J. Herbert Hollomon, "Technology in the United States: Issues for the 1970's," *Technology Review*, June 1972, p. 20; and Seymour Melman, *The Permanent War Economy* (New York: Simon and Schuster, 1974), p. 80.

4. William N. Leonard, "Research and Development in Industrial Growth," *Journal of Political Economy*, March/April 1971, p. 254.

5. See Ibid, p. 250; Hollomon and Harger, "America's Technological Dilemma," p. 38, where these authors refer to figures concerning spin-offs from the defense-space sector to the civilian sector ranging from a low of 5% to a high of 33%; Melman, *The Permanent War Economy*, p. 134, is more pessimistic, maintaining that experts in the Department of Commerce acknowledge only a 5% spin-off; see also Richard Rosenbloom, *Technology Transfer—Process and Policy: An Analysis of the Utilization of Technological By-Products of Military and Space R&D* (Washington, D.C.: National Planning Association, 1965).

6. "Our factories can no longer compete in the technologies of peace because the nation's investment has been so heavy in the technologies of war." See Richard J. Barnet, *Roots of War* (New York: Atheneum, 1972), p. 174.

7. See the insightful remarks by J. Herbert Hollomon in his *Technical Change and American Enterprise* (Washington, D.C.: National Planning Association, October, 1974).

8. Ira C. Magaziner and Robert B. Reich, *Minding America's Business* (New York: Harcourt Brace Jovanovich, Publishers, 1982), p. 228.

9. Ibid, p. 233.

10. The most definitive argument can be found in Melman, *The Permanent War Economy*, especially chapter 4.

11. Seymour Melman, *Pentagon Capitalism* (New York: McGraw Hill Book Company, 1970), p. 10.

12. This close working relationship has for some major military contractors meant less independence. On this point see Adam Yarmolinsky, *The Military Establishment* (New York: Perennial Library, 1973), p. 75. Thus it would seem to follow that the militarized sector of the state also is less independent or autonomous from major military contractors.

13. See James Cypher, "Capitalist Planning and Military Expenditures," *The Review of Radical Political Economics*, Fall 1974, pp. 1–19; and also Michael Reich and David Finkelhor, "Capitalism and the Military Industrial Complex," *The Capitalist System*, eds. Richard C. Edwards et al. (Englewood Cliffs, New Jersey: Prentice Hall, 1972), p. 401, who noted the following: "The fluctuation of military spending has virtually determined the cyclical pattern of the economy."

14. See "Statement of James A. Gray, President, National Machine Tool builders' Association, McLean, Va., Accompanied by Kurt O. Tech, Group Vice President, The Cross Co., Fraser, Mich., and George J. Becker, President and Chief Executive Officer, Giddings and Lewis, Inc., Fond Du Lac, Wis.," made during the *Hearings before the Subcommittee on International Finance of the Committee on Banking, Housing and Urban Affairs*, United States Senate, March 21, 1978 (hereafter, NMBTA Statement, March 21, 1978). Interesting also is the following comment made by Senator Stevenson in the presence of the machine tool industry's representatives during these hearings: "Other countries make it a public policy to have the development of high technology products for export, for civilian purposes. We have never made that an object of American policy. Such support as the Government has provided has been coincidental, by accident, it has been a spinoff of military, space, energy, and other such activities."

2

A Short History of Machine Tool Development and the Industry

This chapter provides a concise history of the American machine tool industry up to the period immediately following the Second World War. However, American machine tool building was taking place well before this industry existed in this country as an independent sector of the economy. Because of this, early American machine tool development will be briefly looked at in this chapter. Though the following discussion pertains almost exclusively to American machine tools and the U.S. machine tool industry, the English contribution to the development of this art will not be overlooked.

A WORD ON MACHINE TOOLS

Progress in industrial societies for over 200 years has been very rapid due in many ways to machine tools. Without machine tools it would have been virtually impossible for industrialization to have occurred in the U.S. or in any other advanced nation. The development of the locomotive, the steam engine, and the steamship, for example, all depended upon machine tools in order to have been built. In short, the development of machine tools marked a great leap forward for mankind and civilization, for they served as a major impetus for industrialization in the U.S., as they did in other modern nations.

Machine tools are not portable by hand, and in time have all become power-driven. They essentially perform extensions of tasks performed by hand tools. Machine tools are classified as those of the metalcutting and metalforming types, both of which shape metal. Basic metalcutting functions are turning, milling, planing, shaping, drilling, boring, grinding, and sawing. Metalforming machine tools, on the other hand, punch, forge, shear, draw, and press metal in the shaping process.[1] Metalcutting tools have been used more than metalforming tools. More data is available on metalcutting tools than on metalforming tools up until the middle of the twentieth century, probably due to their being more widespread and numerous than metalforming tools. For this reason, the discussion in this chapter will be concerned primarily with metalcutting tools, though the Census data cited for 1860 and 1900 below include estimates of both types of tools.

Machine tool development is relatively recent. Modern machine tool development coincided with the Industrial Revolution. James Watt's invention of the steam engine in England in 1776 made use of what has been classified as the first modern machine tool. In fact, this first modern machine tool, developed by John Wilkinson in England in 1775, assured the commercial success of the steam engine which at that time had not yet moved beyond the experimental stage.[2]

EARLY MACHINE TOOL DEVELOPMENT AND BUSINESS IN AMERICA

Machine tool development in America also dates back to the latter part of the eighteenth century. An English mechanic, Samuel Slater, who became known as the father of the American factory system, probably built the first American machine tool for textile production in Rhode Island around 1790. From this time onward, machine tools continued to be developed in America not only for use in textile production but in the manufacturing of cotton also.[3]

Of real importance in the development of early machine tools in America were arms makers. In 1798, Eli Whitney, the inventor of the cotton gin, received a contract from the U.S. government for 12,000 muskets to be completed within a two-year period. Whitney built a number of machine tools in order to produce the muskets. But apparently Whitney encountered problems at his armory close to New Haven, Connecticut on his first government contract, since it actually took him eight years to produce the muskets. His work must have been satisfactory, however, because in 1812 Whitney received another government contract, this time for 15,000 muskets. During his work on this and subsequent contracts, Whitney probably developed, in a very rudimentary and crude form, the system of interchangeable parts.[4]

Not far from Whitney's armory, in the year 1799, Simeon North received a government contract for 500 pistols. By 1800, another 1,500 pistols had been requested by the government. Like Whitney, North's methods involved the use of machine tools which he designed and constructed while making arms for the government. North received another contract from the government in 1813 for 20,000 pistols at a price of seven dollars each. This contract stated that "the component parts of pistols are to correspond so exactly that any limb or part of one Pistol, may be fitted to any other Pistol of the Twenty-Thousand."[5] This was the first government contract that specified that the finished products had to have components that were interchangeable. North developed an extremely close working relationship with the government as an arms builder. This relationship lasted over fifty years, and during this time North's armory produced approximately 50,000 pistols and some 33,000 rifles, all of which involved the use of machine tools.[6]

But the sophistication of the system of interchangeable parts, which led to mass production, is mostly due to the work of John Hall. As a result of Hall's work at Harpers Ferry Armory in West Virginia, the system of interchangeable parts became widespread. In the year 1816 Hall obtained a government contract to produce 100 rifles at twenty-five dollars apiece. Like his counterparts Whitney and North, Hall developed a number of machine tools in order to meet the conditions of his contract with the government. Hall's designing and constructing of machine tools to produce rifles continued to make use of the system of interchangeable parts and eventually his innovative ideas spread across the country.[7]

It must be emphasized that the system of interchangeable parts stemmed from the development of machine tools, government contracts for arms, and the work of Whitney, North, and Hall. At the same time it must be pointed out that machine tools played a very prominent role in building up the government's arsenal of weapons as far back as the latter part of the eighteenth century. The government's dependence on machine tool builders for the construction of arms beginning around 180 years ago indeed is a fact that has not been given adequate attention.

Up until approximately 1840, machine tool development took place largely on an ad hoc basis in America, since individual companies prior to this time did not specialize in this art. When a company needed a particular machine tool it had little choice but to design and build the tool itself. More frequently, mechanics needing machine tools for their work, for example in armories or in textile mills, would design and construct them for their own use. Yet occasionally, when requested, these mechanics would build machine tools for others. The vast majority of the early machine tool building in America by these mechanics occurred in New England, with Rhode Island being the first area of importance.

Between 1800 and 1850 machine tool development began to increase very rapidly in England. Indeed, it does seem to be the case that the art of machine tool building was a bit more advanced in England than in America during the first half of the nineteenth century. This can be maintained given the fact that the upsurge in American machine tool building did not occur, at least for the most part, until a little later, with much of it coming about after 1840. Nonetheless, it is clear that the beginning of modern machine tool development took place almost exclusively in England and America.[8]

Machine tools built in England during the years 1800–1850 were mainly general-purpose tools. For example, the development of the lathe and planer took place in England. In America, during its period of rapid machine tool development, four extremely important tools—the turret lathe, the turret screw machine, the automatic turning lathe, and the universal milling machine—first appeared.

Before discussing the origins of these tools it is important to point out that the invention of the milling machine, a very important machine tool developed in the first quarter of the nineteenth century, has long been attributed to Eli Whitney.[9] More recent historical evidence, however, has determined that a milling machine presumably found in Simeon North's plant had been constructed around 1818—even before the machine discovered in Whitney's gun shop, which was first thought to have been built in 1818 but which now is said to have been constructed in about 1827 (after Whitney's death).[10] (North, as mentioned, had a long-term relationship with the government, beginning in 1799, building arms). But the important advancement of the milling machine, which was essential in improving the system of interchangeable parts, occurred between 1819 and 1826 at Harpers Ferry Armory through the work of John Hall,[11] and then later at other armories, especially at the one in Springfield, Massachusetts. Likewise, gun-producing firms had a major role in improving the milling machine.[12]

In Middlefield, Connecticut, in 1845, Stephen Finch originated the turret lathe under a government contract while producing "percussion locks for an army horse pistol."[13] The development of the universal milling machine also resulted owing to a government contract. Between 1861–1862 the Brown and Sharpe Manufacturing Company produced the first universal milling machine for the Providence Tool Company. The Providence Tool Company had received a government contract at the outbreak of the Civil War to produce Springfield muskets.[14] It is also very significant to note that the very first machine tool sold by Brown and Sharpe of Providence, Rhode Island, one of the initial and largest builders, was a turret screw machine in 1861. Brown and Sharpe made use of this tool originally to design sewing machine parts. But at the outbreak of the Civil War, Brown and Sharpe found other uses for this tool and so it sold its first tool in 1861 to the Providence Tool Company, which, as mentioned, was manufacturing muskets for the government.[15]

H.D. Stone, however, had designed the turret screw machine in 1858. Eventually watches, sewing machines, typewriters, bicycles, locomotives, and later automobiles were being build with the use of this tool. Stemming from Stone's construction of the turret screw machine was the invention of the automatic turret lathe by Christopher Spencer, a former employee of Colt, the gun-making firm, and the designer of the Spencer rifle used in the Civil War by Union troops.[16] This machine in time made automatic all work performed by the lathe. Like the turret screw machine, the automatic turret lathe has been of great importance in the manufacturing of a number of products.

Between the years 1840 and 1880 a number of independent companies producing machinery began to appear in America,[17] though most firms still manufactured other goods. Moreover, the Eighth Census of 1860, for the first time, mentioned machine tools.[18] Prior to this time no Census acknowledged the existence of machine tools in America. So clearly by 1860 the increased demand realized by the newly formed machinery companies was considerable enough to merit designation by the Census Bureau. Contributing enormously to the increased demand for machine tools was the Civil War. During the Civil War (1861–1865), one of the biggest purchasers of machine tools were arms makers. For a leading machine tool company, Brown and Sharpe, arms makers in New England comprised 50% of their total business between September of 1861 until December of 1864.[19] Due to the Civil War there was also an increase in the use of the steam engine, the locomotive, and all kinds of machinery which added even more to the growth in machine tool demand.[20] Whether the Civil War hastened the emergence of independent machine tool firms is unclear. But what is vivid enough is that the Civil War did appreciably increase U.S. machine tool demand which undoubtedly meant technical improvements. The impact of the Civil War on machine tool demand was also felt in Great Britain. For example, for the British tool producing company, Greenwood and Batley, machine tool sales to English arms manufacturers increased phenomenally during the years 1862–1864 as a result of the American Civil War.[21]

From the 1850s to the 1870s the sewing machine also significantly contributed to technical innovations being made on U.S. machine tools.[22] It is reasonable to assume, however, that the stimulus created by the sewing machine for machine tool producers straddled the Civil War years of 1861–1865. The sewing machine and the Civil War, in combination then, engendered an increased demand for machine tools which resulted in the growth of total output during the mid 1800s.

By the 1860s not only had independent companies producing machinery started to appear, but also the building of tools had spread to other areas of the country. New England, as mentioned, was the first important area of machine tool building in America. By 1860, though New England was still the most important general area, machine tool output had grown in the Middle Atlantic States, while Philadelphia had become the major center of production. For some time, Philadelphia remained the leading machine tool building location in the country. Two of the more prominent mechanics in Philadelphia, William Sellers and William Bement, however, first acquired a good deal of their experience in New England and eventually migrated to the city of brotherly love.

The firms in Philadelphia specialized in large metalforming machines, while those in New England produced mostly smaller and lower-priced tools. In 1860, Philadelphia alone accounted for approximately 30% of the total output of metalworking machinery. All of the firms in New England produced some 40% of the metalworking output in 1860, while the states of New York, New Jersey, Maryland, Delaware, and Pennsylvania, excluding Philadelphia, manufactured 25%. Only 5% of the machine tool production at this time occurred in areas west of Pennsylvania.[23]

Machine tool output continued to increase in the 1870s, 1880s, and 1890s. Contributing to this growth in output was the demand for American machine tools abroad during these years. This demand for exports was due mainly to the technical superiority of American machine tools at this time. Moreover, by the later 1880s exports served a very important function, at least for Brown and Sharpe. While in the economic contraction of 1887–1888 Brown and Sharpe's domestic output declined, the company's foreign business more than doubled, reaching almost 50% of its total shipments in 1888. Exports played a similar role for Brown and Sharpe in the economic contractions of 1893–1894 and 1895–1897, when there was a reduction in the company's domestic shipments. The 1895–1897 economic contraction also affected the Bullard Company of Bridgeport, Connecticut, a machine tool firm not quite as large as Brown and Sharpe. Bullard's domestic shipments decreased sharply in 1897, yet there was a more than twofold increase in this year in the company's foreign shipments.[24] Thus despite the general paucity of data on individual machine tool companies during these early years, it does appear to be the case, from the information that is available on Brown and Sharpe and the Bullard Company, that by the latter part of the nineteenth century foreign demand for American machine tools at least partially offset the impact of domestic economic slowdowns.

More railroad track was being laid in the 1880s, than ever before in America. This meant improved and expanded transportation for the country. For machine tool builders, the growth of the railroad meant more business.

During the latter half of the 1880s, machine tool sales noticeably increased to government arsenals, both domestic and foreign. For example, in the quinquenium 1880–1884 Brown and Sharpe produced a total of six machine tools for government arsenals. This changed radically during Brown and Sharpe's next five years of business. Between 1885 and 1889 Brown and Sharpe sold 379 machine tools to government arsenals. There is evidence showing that there occurred a change, not nearly as drastic in the sales of the Bullard Company. Government arsenals bought one machine tool from the Bullard Company during the period 1880–1884. In the next five years, 1885–1889, Bullard's sales to government arsenals increased to ten machine tools.[25]

Government arsenals continued to be very big purchasers of machine tools from Brown and Sharpe in the early years of the 1890s, even though they bought much less than they did in the last five years of the 1880s. Machine tools sold to government arsenals by the Bullard Company grew markedly to forty-nine in the period 1890–1894 from the ten it had sold in the preceding five years.[26] Thus, though all the data is not available, government arsenals probably created additional demand for other machine tool companies also, beginning at least by the 1890s. Also during the 1890s, the electrical equipment and the bicycle industries began to greatly stimulate machine tool demand.

But it was the bicycle industry that was the biggest boon to machine tool business. Throughout the 1890s and continuing until around 1909, the bicycle industry grew at an exceptionally fast pace. As a result, for close to two decades, the bicycle industry was the most sustained consumer of machine tools. At this time women discovered that they too had legs, and so in many ways the "bicycle doomed the Victorian era."[27] Along with the increased demand for machine tools created by the bicycle industry, tool producing companies also made a number of technological innovations and improvements on equipment, such as the grinding machine.[28]

Exactly when the machine tool industry could be classified as constituting an independent sector of the U.S. economy is a debatable issue. If one takes the formation of the National Machine Tool Builders' Association in Cleveland, Ohio in 1902 as an indicator, then the beginning of the twentieth century would mark the birth of this industry. What is more, the National Machine Tool Builders' Association has published no data on years prior to 1901. Yet it is true that the *American Machinist*, a trade journal on metalworking equipment, published its first issue in November 1877, which does suggest the rudiments of an independent machine tool industry. And on June 28, 1879 the *American Machinist* listed machine tool companies in existence at that time which comprised what this journal termed "a distinct branch of industry."[29] In any event, it is clear that no distinct machine tool industry existed in America prior to 1877. And 1902 is certainly the latest date for recognizing the existence of the U.S. machine tool industry. So although pinpointing the first year of the American machine tool industry's existence is not very likely at all, it is correct to say that this industry definitely emerged during the years 1877 to 1902.

The emergence of the machine tool industry at this time is important since it was probably advantageous to the endurance of the industry. It seems that the merger movement beginning in the 1890s and continuing to the early 1900s had little effect on the emerging machine tool industry. This merger movement was characterized by mergers that were mostly "horizontal" in nature, or, in other words, that removed competitors from the market. Since the machine tool industry was only just emerging during the time when this merger movement was taking place, the elimination of competitors was not a matter of much importance to most tool builders.

THE U.S. MACHINE TOOL INDUSTRY ENTERING THE TWENTIETH CENTURY

Up until 1880 the vast majority of machine tool building in America took place in the New England and the Middle Atlantic

States. During the 1880s, Ohio became an important area for machine tool building. Machine tool building continued to push westward, due at least in part to the concentration of companies in the East. The Middle Western States, by 1900, accounted for the majority of machine tool building in the country. The fact that the formation of the National Machine Tool Builders' Association was in Cleveland, Ohio also signifies the growing importance of the Midwestern States to this industry. According to Ross Robertson's estimates of metalworking output in 1900, the Midwestern States accounted for 34% of the total, with Ohio alone making up 29% while in the Middle Atlantic States, production had declined to 26% and the New England States made up approximately 30% of the total output.[30] Though by 1900 Cincinnati, Ohio had become the country's leading machine tool producing area, Philadelphia at this time was only slightly behind. Yet as the 1900s wore on, Philadelphia's importance steadily declined as a major machine tool producing center. And so at the expense of Philadelphia, and also the entire Middle Atlantic region and the New England States, the Midwest became (and remained) the nation's leading machine tool producing area.

The first decade of the twentieth century witnessed the phenomenal growth of the automobile industry. As the bicycle declined in importance to the machine tool industry, the automobile became a welcomed substitute in regard to demand.[31] Soon the automobile industry became the largest single purchaser of machine tools up until World War I. Much of the machine tool development that took place for the bicycle industry was easily transferred and adapted to the requirements of the automobile industry. For example, machine tool companies made technical improvements on the grinding machine for the bicycle industry. Automobile production also required grinding machines, although more advanced ones. As a result, machine tool companies technically improved the grinding machine for the automobile industry. Other major machine tool improvements or innovations occurred in milling, in tapping, in the lathe, and in drilling owing to the enormous growth of the automobile industry. In short, the automobile paved the way for a number of technical improvements and innovations in machine tools while also greatly stimulating the demand for them, as no other product had done before in America.[32]

Yet the machine tool industry still had to contend with the business cycle. In each of the four periods of economic contraction from 1902 to 1914 there was a decline in domestic machine tool shipments. To some extent exports helped to cushion the impact of these recessions on the machine tool industry. Nonetheless, declines in machine tool business during periods of economic slowdowns were very problematic to builders during the early years of the twentieth century.

WORLD WAR I AND THE U.S. MACHINE TOOL INDUSTRY

To a much greater extent than even the automobile industry had done before, World War I, 1914–1918, enormously increased machine tool demand. As indicated above, there has historically been a rather close relationship between the production of arms and machine tools. So when World War I began, and because of the superiority of U.S. machine tools, there was an unprecedented increase in the demand for American tools. This increased demand was met by the relatively numerous machine tool firms that by 1914 totaled 409,[33] most of which were small and middle-sized companies.

Though the U.S. did not enter World War I until 1917, still-increasing demand resulting from it had, by 1915, caused shipments of American machine tools to climb from $35.3 million in 1914 to $103.4 million in the following year. Contributing to this increase in demand were machine tool exports to the Allies in Europe. U.S. machine tool exports grew from $14 million in 1914 to $28 million in 1915.[34]

Shipments of American machine tools reached their peak in 1918. The value of American machine tool shipments in 1918 was $220.6 million. Prior to World War I the biggest single year for shipments of U.S. machine tools was $44.6 million in 1913. Thus by 1918 U.S. machine tool shipments had increased by almost five times from their highest point reached before World War I.

Uninterrupted production in the automobile industry remained beneficial to machine tool companies until 1917. Factory sales of passenger cars reached nearly 1.8 million in 1917. In 1918, the War Industries Board, created in July of 1917, instructed the automobile industry to cut back production of passenger cars for civilian use and instead manufacture more vehicles needed for the war. Moreover, during the conflict the automobile industry produced war materiel such as tractors, shells, gun carriages, guns, and aircraft engines.[35] Stepped-up production in the automobile industry stimulated to a large extent by the war, in short, contributed to the soaring business of machine tool companies.

The aircraft industry's growth during World War I also increased the sales of machine tool companies. The aircraft industry in 1916 produced 411 planes, but by 1917 the number grew to 2,148. More significantly, in 1918 the production of planes by the aircraft industry climbed to 14,020, of which 13, 991 were for the military.[36] Clearly such a large volume of planes being manufactured that required many machine tools in order to be produced greatly increased the output of the machine tool industry.

Increasing output in the automobile, aircraft, and other manufacturing industries producing war materiel led to the machine tool industry's operating at capacity toward the end of 1918. Yet it is clear that the machine tool industry met the requirements of increased production during World War I.[37] In order to satisfy the unusually high demand for machine tools during the war, the ten-hour day became common for a good many workers in tool producing firms.[38] To help with this upsurge of business, machine tool companies hired a significant number of women during World War I. Some 5,000 women were working in machine tool companies by 1918. Although women made up about 12% of the workers in machine tool companies at this time, a little less than half of all females were actually on the production lines, since most were performing clerical or related tasks.[39]

But the war could not last forever, and machine tool builders were cognizant of this. The exceptionally good business realized by machine tool firms during the war sooner or later had to come to an end. In this respect, machine tool builders were certain that reduced demand for their products was inevitable once the war was over. So not without foresight, machine tool builders, during the midst of the war, began considering what would happen to their industry when the fighting ended. Machine tool builders attempted to protect their war-generated business by writing "no cancellation" clauses into their contracts. Tool builders hoped that such actions would lessen the anticipated reduction in demand for their products following World War I.[40]

Another move made by machine tool builders to cushion their business from reduced demand was an attempt to keep prices up as much as possible after the war. Toward the end of the war the prices of machine tools increased faster than costs. Machine tool companies wanted to maintain these large profit margins, or at least as much of them as possible, following the war. Nonetheless, decreased demand after the war necessitated a decline in prices for some tools, something that most builders expected despite their hopes to prevent this from happening.[41]

Machine tool shipments fell in 1919 by $59.9 million from the previous year. Machine tool shipments declined once again in 1920, this time more modestly by $9.5 million. Without the added stimulus of war production, the machine tool industry had to contend with a postwar slump. Thus the end of World War I and the retrenchment of military expenditures had brought with it a diminution in the business activity of the machine tool industry.

For the machine tool firm the National Acme Manufacturing Company of Cleveland, Ohio (later, in 1968, merging with the Cleveland Twist Drill Company to become the Acme-Cleveland Corporation), the end of World War I created an additional problem of some consequence. Since it is very likely that at least some other tool building companies had to contend with a similar misfortune, the following occurrence pertaining to the National Acme Manufacturing Company is especially interesting to note. During World War I, the demand for Gridley machines, named after their designer George Gridley, increased tremendously. But the surfeit of Gridley machines, also called multiple spindle automatic machines, could not be sold after the war because of the general reduction of machine tool demand. According to an official of the Acme-Cleveland Corporation, Arthur Armstrong, in his historical account of the National Acme Manufacturing Company at the end of the First World War, "the company was caught with a large inventory of machines and no capital. Deep financial troubles followed, almost wrecking the company."[42]

THE INTERWAR YEARS

Despite the weakening of machine tool demand after the war, business was better than expected for many tool producing companies. But it was certainly not the aircraft industry that saved machine tool companies from a much bigger loss of business. From a peak of over 14,000 planes built during the war in 1918, production in the aircraft industry by 1920 had fallen to just a little over 300 units. What mostly did benefit machine tool companies in the early postwar years was the automobile industry. Immediately following the First World War there was a resumption in the sales of passenger cars, which, as mentioned, had been cut back in 1918. New car sales climbed to more than 1.6 million in 1919, an increase of over 700,000 from the preceding year; in 1920, new car sales amounted to more than 1.9 million. This increase in the sales of passenger motor vehicles indeed prevented machine tool demand from taking a deeper plunge at this time.

The recession of 1920–1921 pushed machine tool production down to about what it was in 1914. Factory sales of new automobiles dropped off in 1921 and quite naturally this hurt the machine tool industry. But by 1922 auto sales were back up once again and this meant improved business for the machine tool industry. Also contributing to machine tool demand was the radio industry, which at this time was growing very rapidly.[43]

Machine tool demand for the next five years depended heavily on the automobile industry. (And the growth in machine tool output in the Middle West during the 1920s was mainly the result of the automobile industry being located in this part of the country.) Yet it is true that the railroad, farm equipment, appliance, radio, and machinery industries also were important contributors to the business of machine tool companies, but to a lesser degree. In 1928, aircraft production significantly increased for the first time since the war. About 25% of the growth in aircraft output was due to the production of planes for the military. The year 1928 was also the machine tool industry's best year so far in the 1920s.

Sales of passenger cars reached their all-time high, 4.5 million, in 1929. Though still relatively small, the aircraft industry produced 6,193 planes in 1929, mostly for civilian purposes. This was the largest output of planes since the war for the aircraft industry. With both the automobile and the aircraft industries doing well, machine tool shipments in 1929 were the highest they had been since 1918.

On Black Tuesday, October 29, 1929, the stock market crashed. Soon the worse depression ever struck the U.S. Machine tool production was slow to decline, however, mainly owing to the strength of new car sales, and, to a much lesser extent, the aircraft industry. Yet due to the severely depressed state of the economy, both automobile and aircraft production dropped off sharply over the next few years. Between 1929 and 1932 factory sales of passenger cars declined by 75%. For the aircraft industry, during the period 1929–1933, production fell by 78%. These depressed conditions in turn adversely affected machine tool shipments. By 1932, machine tool shipments declined to $22 million, the lowest they had been since 1908.

It is very important to note that the machine tool industry survived another merger movement which began in the 1920s and lasted about ten years. Unlike the merger movement that started in the 1890s, mergers taking place during the 1920s were largely "vertical." That is, many companies at this time were not concerned with absorbing their competitors, as they were in the previous merger movement. Rather, their concern was in merging with suppliers and with retail distributors. Machine tool companies, though suppliers of important capital goods, were probably considered bad economic ventures due to the very cyclical nature of machine tool business, which had been demonstrated frequently by the time of the depression.

Economic recovery was slow in the U.S. after the depression. Indeed, it is more accurate to say that full recovery never really occurred until World War II. For the machine tool industry, business was especially sluggish until 1936. Even with new car sales turning upward once again by 1933, this did little good for the suffering machine tool industry. The very hard times that the machine tool industry experienced in the first part of the 1930s as a result of the depression were reflected in the *American Machinist* inventory of metalworking equipment taken in 1935. This inventory pointed out that 65% of all American machine tools were over ten years of age, while only 48% were this old five years earlier.[44] In short, largely because of the depression, during the first part of the 1930s American businesses were not buying many new machine tools, and tool producing companies suffered enormously from, what was for them, a dire reality.

By 1936, the government once again began pump priming the aircraft industry by placing new orders for military planes. Sizeable orders for military planes continued to be placed in 1937. This resulted in an extremely good year of business in 1937 for the aircraft industry.[45] This was also the best year for the automobile industry thus far in the 1930s. With noticeable improvements in the automobile and the aircraft industries, along with a moderately growing economy, shipments of machine tools understandably increased in 1937.

But the rug was quickly pulled from underneath the feet of machine tool builders in 1938. Another recession had caused machine tool production to be reduced by some $50 million in 1938 from the previous year. Yet all was not bad for machine tool builders. Apart from the years 1932 and 1933, American machine tool exports had grown in importance to many companies during the 1930s. Owing to this fact, there is no question that, given the adverse impact of the domestic recession on the machine tool industry, the growth in exports between 1937 and 1938 was extremely advantageous to builders. A 67% increase in machine tool exports from 1937 to 1938 undoubtedly reduced the impact of this recession on tool producing companies.

WORLD WAR II AND THE U.S. MACHINE TOOL INDUSTRY

Recovery for the machine tool industry after the recession of 1937–1938 began in 1939. Total shipments of machine tools returned to about the level they had been at in 1937. While exports of American machine tools continued to grow in 1939 and 1940, domestic demand also showed signs of significant improvement. The flagging economy of most of the 1930s had been partly revitalized by 1940, to some extent due to the fighting in Europe, and this resulted in an amelioration in domestic business for the machine tool industry. Moreover, the war in Europe was also directly beneficial to American builders since it increased U.S. machine tool exports.

Factory sales of automobiles increased in 1939 and grew even more by 1940. As before, a thriving automobile industry was beneficial to machine tool companies. But even more important to machine tool companies during the years 1939–1945 was the rapidly expanding aircraft industry that had been gaining momentum since 1936, in large part due to military orders for planes. Aircraft production totaled 5,856 planes in 1939, over a third of which were for the military. The aircraft industry reached its peak in 1944 producing 95,272 planes, and every one of these was for the military. Moreover, during the war years the foremost manufacturing sector in the country was the aircraft industry. This is indicated by virtue of the fact that a total of 8,780 machine tools were in place in the aircraft industry in 1940; by 1945 there were 276,466 machine tools located in the aircraft industry—the largest increase out of all U.S. industries during this period.[46] War expenditures were therefore decisive in the maturation of the aircraft industry and, consequently, the demand for machine tools grew tremendously.

Perhaps nothing was as clear to machine tool builders than that war production meant extremely good times for them. This was so since tool builders were very cognizant of the fact that the nation's military strength was initially contingent upon machine tools, for without them it would be exceedingly difficult to manufacture weapons and war materiel. The government, likewise, understood this to be true. In fact, even before the war, both the Army and Navy made it very clear that they realized the importance of machine tools in the event of a national emergency.[47] In the early part of World War II, William S. Knudsen, Director-General of the Office of Production Management (which was succeeded by the War Production Board), stated that "machine tools are the most essential item in the defense program . . . they are needed for the production of all kinds of munitions."[48] The comment made by George C. Marshall, Chief of Staff during the Second World War, is also worth noting: "Practically every problem concerned with the production of arms and equipment, ships and planes, starts with the question of machine tools. The tool builders, therefore, constitute the keystone of the entire procurement structure."[49] In short, the mutual recognition of the importance of machine tools for war production resulted in a close relationship between the government and the machine tool industry during World War II. However, this direct relationship arose only because of the war (and, as we shall see in subsequent chapters, it did not endure with the same intensity throughout the postwar years).

With aircraft production consuming the largest number of new machine tools during the war, the importance of the automobile to tool builders steadily declined. Soon after the U.S. entered the war in 1941, the production of automobiles for civilian purposes came to a halt. But this was not due to an ebullient sense of patriotism on the part of automobile manufacturers. Rather, the automobile industry had been forced to convert to war production; by June of 1942 nearly 70% of its machine tools were being used for military purposes.[50]

The war had created an unprecedented demand for new machine tools. Apart from aircraft production, thousands of new machine tools were developed for munitions and other war essentials. Demand for machine tools was so great during World War II that the industry had a difficult time satisfying it. This was true despite the fact that the machine tool industry expanded its plant, subcontracted some of its work, and made use of multiple shifts and overtime for workers, while at the same time new tool building companies entered the field.[51]

Nevertheless, according to the National Machine Tool Builders' Association, during World War II the industry did build more than one million machine tools for defense contractors. This amount was more than the total number of machine tools produced by the industry in the forty years prior to the war,[52] and it accounted for about 90% of the metalcutting machine tool shipments during the period 1940–1945. A very good indication of the impact World War II had on the industry can be obtained from looking at machine tool shipments and employment during these years. Machine tool shipments had increased more than six times to $132 billion, with the vast majority of the tools being used in the U.S. In regard to employment, in 1939 metalcutting tool builders employed less than 40,000 workers; by 1942, the number of jobs increased to 120,000.[53]

THE AFTERMATH OF WORLD WAR II

One direct result of World War II was the many new machine tools built during the period 1940–1945. The country had a very large number of young machine tools by 1945 relative to what it had in 1940. Thirty-three percent of all U.S. machine tools in 1940 were less than ten years of age; by the end of the war in 1945, 62% of all American machine tools were under ten years of age.[54] Thus not only did the war have a catalytic effect on the machine tool industry by greatly increasing demand, but it also left the country with a fairly young stock of tools.

As in World War I, machine tool builders knew very well that once the war was over demand for their products would take a turn for the worse. Beginning in 1945 aircraft production significantly decreased from the previous year. The enormous demand for machine tools occasioned by aircraft production during the war was rapidly coming to an end. The automobile industry did not compensate for the reduced postwar demand for machine tools as it did after World War I. Factory sales of passenger cars did not amount to anything much until 1946. With aircraft output decreasing in 1945, and with the automobile industry slow in making the transition from war to civilian production, the demand for machine tools declined. Above all else, it was clear to machine tool builders in 1945 that very little could be done to prevent a significant reduction in the sales of new tools.

Exacerbating the reduction of machine tool demand after the war, apart from decreased military spending, was another major problem. This problem was the competition the machine tool industry encountered from the government. By 1945, the government owned one-third of the nation's machine tools. Like private businesses, the government had also increased its purchasing of new machine tools during the Second World War. The government wanted to dispose of these machine tools as quickly as possible by selling them at low prices so as to hasten the transition to civilian production and to counter inflationary tendencies following the war.[55]

Despite the state's intention to assist American businesses after the war, the machine tool industry suffered because of the sale of government-owned tools. Lower prices for used but still relatively young government tools were harmful to machine tool builders. This was so since by underselling the machine tool industry the government became its competitor in the market.[56] Evidently the competition from the government did have a fairly big impact on the machine tool industry since production and shipments continued to decline until 1950.[57]

Thus, the combined effects of the enormous retrenchment of military expenditures along with the competition from the government in regard to the selling off of its used tools pushed the machine tool industry into a slump following World War II. Aggravating even more the machine tool industry's postwar slump was the recession of 1948–1949. Even with exports strong during the early postwar years and with little import threat, the machine tool industry faced bad times until military expenditures increased during the Korean War. This meant that increased aircraft production and other war materiel once again created additional machine tool demand.

But the machine tool industry did have one happy experience in the early postwar years. Metalforming firms became part of the National Machine Tool Builders' Association in 1947. Prior to this time the National Machine Tool Builders' Association consisted of only metalcutting firms. Yet the enlargement of the National Machine Tool Builders' Association had virtually no effect in combatting the military-engendered business decline experienced by both metalforming and metalcutting firms in the early postwar years. Nor did the enlargement of the National Machine Tool Builders' Association help to lessen the impact of recession on the industry, as the economic downturn of 1948–1949 made clear.

CONCLUSION

Though this chapter is in no way meant to be an exhaustive account of machine tools or the industry itself, it presents three major factors that tend to be notable in the history of tool building in America. The first major point to note is that arms, textile manufacturing, the sewing machine, the bicycle, and the automobile were very decisive to machine tool builders in respect to both technical innovations and demand for their products. During the two world wars, the aircraft industry served a similar purpose for machine tool builders, while between these two wars its importance tended to vary at different times.

The second critical issue concerns arms making and military materiel. As noted, arms builders made significant contributions to early machine tool development in America. Later, government arsenals began purchasing machine tools in large quantities which increased demand. During both World War I and World War II, demand for machine tools increased tremendously. Following both of these wars the machine tool industry experienced a decline in business activity.

After the First World War the automobile saved the machine tool industry from an even worse reduction in business, and by the end of the 1920s aircraft production also began to become more important to tool producing companies. But the period after World War II was much different for the machine tool industry. Automobile-induced demand for machine tools was noticeably small at first. Of real importance was the fact that the massive reduction in military expenditures and the concomitant decline in aircraft production after the war critically weakened machine tool demand. Also adding to the misery of the machine tool industry was the government's selling of used machines after 1945. In short, it is very evident that during the Second World War the machine tool industry became very dependent on military spending, and subsequently, when these expenditures were cut back, there was no compensating private-sector demand available to stabilize the machine tool industry until the Korean War.

Thus over time, from the early arms makers to the Second World War, machine tool builders eventually (that is, by 1945) developed a dependence on military demand. The years between World War II and the Korean War provide indisputable evidence as to the strength of this dependence. Machine tool demand, because it was too dependent on military spending during the Second World War, could only be adequately stimulated through another war. The outbreak of the Korean War in 1950 soon provided this necessary stimulus to machine tool demand.

Lastly, an issue of grave importance to machine tool builders since the end of the nineteenth century has been the slowing down of the economy. Economic contractions have hurt machine tool demand. Indeed, throughout the first half of the twentieth century economic downturns had been the machine tool industry's most damaging problem. Yet U.S. machine tool exports clearly played a role in lessening the intensity of economic contractions on tool producing companies from the end of the last century up until after the Second World War.

NOTES

1. National Machine Tool Builders' Association (booklet), *Machine Tools/New Concepts for a New Day*; National Machine Tool Builders' Association (booklet), *Machine Tools/America's Muscles*.

2. "Machine Tools," *Machinery's Encyclopedia*, IV (New York: The Industrial Press, 1917), pp. 278–79.

3. Ibid., p. 281

4. "Metalworking: Yesterday and Tomorrow," *American Machinist* (100th Anniversary Issue), November 1977, p. B–6.

5. Ibid., p. B–8.

6. Ibid.

7. Ibid., p. B–12.

8. "Machine Tools," *Machinery's Encyclopedia*, p. 278.

9. See, for example, the booklet published by the National Machine Tool Builders' Association, *Machine Tools/New Concepts for a New Day*.

10. "Metalworking: Yesterday and Tomorrow," *American Machinist*, pp. B–7 and B–8.

11. Ibid., p. B–8.

12. Nathan Rosenberg, "Technological Change in the Machine Tool Industry, 1840–1910," *The Journal of Economic History*, December 1963, p. 428.·

13. Ibid., p. 423; see "Metalworking: Yesterday and Tomorrow," *American Machinist*, p. D–12, for a discussion of Stephen Finch as the originator of the turret lathe.

14. Duncan M. McDougall, "Machine Tool Output, 1861–1910," *Output, Employment, and Productivity in the United States after 1800, Studies*

in Income and Wealth, vol. 30 (New York: National Bureau of Economic Research, 1966), p. 500.

15. Ibid.

16. Rosenberg, "Technological Change in the Machine Tool Industry, 1840–1910," p. 429; "Metalworking: Yesterday and Tomorrow," *American Machinist*, p. D–8.

17. Rosenberg, "Technological Change in the Machine Tool Industry, 1840–1910," p. 418.

18. Ross M. Robertson, "Changing Production of Metalworking Machinery, 1860–1920," *Output, Employment, and Productivity in the United States after 1800, Studies in Income and Wealth*, vol,. 30 (New York: National Bureau of Economic Research, 1966), p. 480.

19. McDougall, "Machine Tool Output, 1861–1910," p. 506.

20. "Metalworking: Yesterday and Tomorrow," *American Machinist*, p. C–16.

21. Roderick Floud, *The British Machine Tool Industry, 1850–1914* (London: Cambridge University Press, 1976), pp. 158 and 163.

22. Rosenberg, "Technological Change in the Machine Tool Industry, 1840–1910," p. 430.

23. Robertson, "Changing Production of Metalworking Machinery, 1860–1920," pp. 487–88. Estimates include both metalforming and metalcutting tools.

24. McDougall, "Machine Tool Output, 1861–1910," p. 517, table A–3. The data for the Brown and Sharpe Manufacturing Company and the Bullard Company deal only with metalcutting tools.

25. Ibid., p. 505, table 2.

26. Ibid.

27. "Metalworking: Yesterday and Tomorrow," *American Machinist*, p. D–1.

28. Rosenberg, "Technological Change in the Machine Tool Industry, 1840–1910," pp. 434–36. Brown and Sharpe first developed the grinding machine for use on the sewing machine.

29. Robertson, "Changing Production of Metalworking Machinery, 1860–1920," p. 484.

30. Ibid., p. 482. The other 10% of metalworking output at this time occurred in the remaining tool producing areas.

31. By 1909, factory sales of passenger cars (factory sales are close to the actual number produced) were 123,900, the highest they had ever been thus far, and almost twice as large as they were in 1908. This and subsequent data on factory sales of passenger cars in this chapter are from the U.S. Bureau of the Census, *Historical Statistics of the United States, Colonial Times to 1970, Bicentennial Edition*, Washington, D.C., 1975, p. 716.

32 Rosenberg, "Technological Change in the Machine Tool Industry, 1840–1910," pp. 434–39.

33. Ibid., p. 421.

34. Estimated data on machine tool shipments (close to the actual number produced) and exports used here and subsequently in this chapter are from Harless D. Wagoner, *The U.S. Machine Tool Industry from 1900 to 1950* (Cambridge, Massachusetts: The M.I.T. Press, 1968), table 6, pp. 362–63. These data include only metalcutting tools.

35. "Metalworking: Yesterday and Tomorrow," *American Machinist*, p. E.16.

36. Data in this chapter on aircraft production, including planes manufactured for the military, are from the U.S. Bureau of the Census, *Historical Statistics of the United States, Colonial Times to 1970, Bicentennial Edition*, Washington, D.C., 1975, p. 768.

37. James A. Gray, "Machine Tool Exports: A Smaller Slice of the Pie," p. 2. This was an address given to the Annual Forecasting Conference of the National Machine Tool Builders' Association on September 19, 1979.

38. "Metalworking: Yesterday and Tomorrow," *American Machinist*, p. E–16.

39. Wagoner, *The U.S. Machine Tool Industry from 1900 to 1950*, p,. 104.

40. Ibid. p. 142.

41. Ibid., pp. 142–43.

42. Arthur S. Armstrong, "The Persistence of Struggle: The Story of the Acme Cleveland Corporation," p. 15. This is an address that was given by Arthur Armstrong, former chairman and chief executive officer of the Acme-Cleveland Corporation, in 1976 to the Newcomen Society.

43. "Metalworking: Yesterday and Tomorrow," *American Machinist*, p. F–7.

44. Ibid., p. F–8.

45. Indeed, even though defense spending did not amount to too much during the twenties and thirties, the aircraft industry, along with other weapons contractors, nonetheless, developed a close working relationship with the military during the interwar years. "Despite the relatively small defense budgets of the 1920's and 1930's, the pattern of industrial-military relations during those years foreshadows in many striking ways what developed after World War II." See Paul A. Koistinen, "The 'Industrial-Military Complex' in Historical Perspective: The Interwar Years," *The Journal of American History*, March 1970, p. 820.

46. See Bradley Stoughton, *History of the Tools Division, War Production Board* (New York: McGraw-Hill Book Company, Inc ., 1949) table 1, p. 81.

47. Ibid., p. 2; Wagoner, *The U.S. Machine Tool Industry from 1900 to 1950*, p. 233.

48.National Machine Tool Builders' Association (booklet), *Machine Tools/Basic to the Nation.*

49. Quoted in "Statement of the National Machine Tool Builders' Association, Henry D. Sharpe, Jr., First Vice President," made during the *Hearing before the Committee on Ways and Means*, House of Representatives, June 4, 1970 (hereafter, NMTBA Statement, June 4, 1970).

50. Wagoner, *The U.S. Machine Tool Industry from 1900 to 1950*, pp. 240 and 325.

51. Ibid., chapter 8.

52. National Machine Tool Builders' Association (booklet), *Machine Tools/Basic to the Nation.*

53. Figures on employment from Stoughton, *History of the Tools Division, War Production Board*, p. 7.

54. "The 11th American Machinist Inventory of Metalworking Equipment 1973," *American Machinist*, October 29, 1973, p. 143.

55. Wagoner, *The U.S. Machine Tool Industry from 1900 to 1950*, pp. 318–19.

56. Cf. with Otto E. Hintz, James H. Sullivan and Robert C. Van Parys, *Machine Tool Industry Study: Final Report* (Rock Island, Illinois: U.S. Army Industrial Base Engineering Activity, November 1, 1978) p. 26.

57. "In effect, the government flooded the market, which forced many units of the machine tool industry out of business. In all some 235,000 surplus machines, about seven times the total produced in 1938, were sold. Partly because of these surplus sales, the market broke completely." James G. Abert and Clayton McCuistion, *The Defense Dependency of the Metalworking Machinery and Equipment Industry and Disarmament Implications* (Bethesda, Maryland: Resource Management Corporation, May 1969), p. 24.

3

The Industry: Its Structure and Problems

This chapter will examine the structural characteristics and condition of the U.S. machine tool industry during the years after World War II. Structural characteristics are those features which together distinguish the machine tool industry from others in the U.S., such as its size, location, capital investments, and the amount of research and development. This chapter will also incorporate at times a comparative analysis of the U.S. machine tool industry with its foreign competitors, but mainly those in Japan and West Germany.

A DESCRIPTIVE PROFILE OF THE U.S. MACHINE TOOL INDUSTRY

The U.S. machine tool industry is comparatively small, that is, relative to many other industries in America. In fact, the entire machine tool industry (including both metalcutting and metalforming firms) is smaller than most of the big companies in the U.S. The vast majority of the top 100 companies on *Fortune's* list of the 500 leading industrial firms in the U.S. have individual assets that exceed those of all the machine tool industry. And compared to the really giant companies like General Motors and Exxon, the machine tool industry is minute. For example, the gross assets of the machine tool industry in 1981 were $2.263 billion while the total assets of General Motors and Exxon in this same year were $38.991 billion and $62.931 billion respectively.[1]

Although it is relatively small, the machine tool industry is a very basic capital-goods producing industry. Directly or indirectly, machine tools have a part in manufacturing and transporting all products. So notwithstanding the size of the industry, "machine tools can be considered the keystone of modern industrial processes."[2]

A large number of small- and medium-sized firms make up the U.S. machine tool industry. Few machine tool firms are large. Many machine tool firms are still privately owned, though the larger ones are listed as public companies. It is not at all uncommon to find in a machine tool company more than one official with the same last name. In fact, in a few of the smaller firms all of the company officials have the same last name.[3] Even in the largest U.S. machine tool firm, Cincinnati Milacron, Inc., a publicly owned company, there is family control. The chief executive officer of Cincinnati Milacron, James Geier, is the grandson of the man who in 1887 began the business as a tool shop. Over 25% of the shares of Cincinnati Milacron in 1971 were held by the Geier family.[4]

Establishments that are part of the machine tool industry principally produce metalcutting and metalforming tools. The machine tool industry has grown during the postwar years in regard to the number of establishments comprising it. Throughout the postwar years metalcutting establishments have consistently outnumbered metalforming ones by more than two times. As can be seen from Table 1, the actual number of machine tool establishments has always been quite large.

Not all machine tool companies are members of the National Tool Builders' Association (NMTBA). Only a little more than 350 companies are members of the NMTBA, an organization which represents the industry politically. According to the NMTBA, all of its members combined produce approximately 90% of the machine tool output in the U.S.[5]

Because of the large number of small and medium-sized firms, concentration of the machine tool industry's employment amongst the bigger firms has been very evident. A relatively small number of big machine tool establishments during the postwar years have employed a sizeable number of workers. On the other hand, fewer individuals have worked in each of the many small and medium-sized establishments. For example, in 1967, twenty-five establishments (out of 1,253), with 1,000 or more workers each, accounted for 41% of the industry's total

Table 1. Number of Machine Tool Establishments, 1958–1982

Year	Metalcutting	Metalforming	Total
1958	627	291	918
1963	801	366	1,167
1967	903	350	1,253
1972	894	383	1,277
1977	919	426	1,345
1982	941	452	1,393

Sources: Data for 1958-1972 from the U.S. Bureau of the Census, 1972 Census of Manufactures; data for 1977 and 1982 from the U.S. Bureau of the Census, 1982 Census of Manufactures (preliminary reports on metalcutting and metalforming machine tools, July 1984).

Note: The number of machine tool establishments is actually higher than the number of companies because a few firms have more than one establishment. In 1982 there were 860 metalcutting companies and 430 metalforming companies.

employment. Not only did the rest of the establishments in 1967 employ less than 1,000 individuals each, but the majority of them (77%) had fewer than fifty workers each. Looking just at the more numerous metalcutting builders in 1972, an estimated 40% of all metalcutting workers held jobs in nine establishments (out of 894) employing over 1,000 individuals each. In this same year, nearly 70% of all metalcutting establishments employed less than twenty workers each.[6]

The fact that a large number of workers have been employed by the bigger establishments strongly suggests economic concentration within the machine tool industry. But even more indicative in regard to economic concentration within the machine tool industry is the number of employees and shipments of different-sized establishments. The data indicate that a few big establishments with a very large payroll do a quite sizeable share of the industry's business. For example, seven big metalcutting establishments in 1972, employing on the average between 1,000 and 2,499 workers each, had shipments valued higher than the combined total of 800 smaller establishments with less than 100 workers each.[7] In the 1977 Census the seven big metalcutting establishments' share of total shipments had declined somewhat; nevertheless, the total value of their shipments was higher than the combined total of 822 smaller establishments employing less than 100 workers each. Only twenty-six metalcutting establishments out of 917 listed in 1977 accounted for nearly 50% of the reported shipments and more than half of all reported metalcutting employment. (See Table 2).

A listing of machine tool companies according to their sales would vary from one year to the next. However, the following list represents twelve of the major machine tool companies in the U.S.:

Cincinnati Milacron, Inc.	The Monarch Machine Tool Company
Cross & Trecker	Brown and Sharpe Manufacturing Company
Litton Industries	Houdaille Industries, Inc.
Giddings & Lewis, Inc.	White Consolidated Industries

Table 2. Concentration within the Machine Tool Industry, 1977

Metalcutting Establishments				
Establishments with an average of:	Number of Employees	Number of Establishments	Value of Shipments (million dollars)	
1 to 4 employees	600	315	24.6	(.9%)
5 to 9 employees	1,200	184	48.3	(1.7%)
10 to 19 employees	1,500	112	63.4	(2.2%)
20 to 49 employees	4,400	144	193.3	(6.9%)
50 to 99 employees	4,600	67	217.5	(7.7%)
100 to 249 employees	6,300	40	321.0	(11.4%)
250 to 499 employees	10,300	28	562.9	(20.0%)
500 to 999 employees	13,800	19	726.2	(25.8%)
1,000 to 2,499 employees	16,600	7	655.6	(23.3%)
2,500 employees or more	(D)	1	(D)	
Totals	59,400	917	2,812.7	(99.9%)*

Metalforming Establishments				
Establishments with an average of:	Number of Employees	Number of Establishments	Value of Shipments (million dollars)	
1 to 4 employees	200	119	9.9	(.9%)
5 to 9 employees	500	78	24.2	(2.1%)
10 to 19 employees	900	66	42.0	(3.7%)
20 to 49 employees	2,300	75	107.4	(9.5%)
50 to 99 employees	2,100	31	97.4	(8.6%)
100 to 249 employees	5,200	35	250.1	(22.1%)
250 to 499 employees	4,500	13	235.7	(20.8%)
500 to 999 employees	7,900	8	364.0	(32.2%)
1,000 to 2,499 employees	(D)	1	(D)	
Totals	23,700	426	1,130.6	(99.9%)

Source: U.S. Bureau of the Census, 1977 Census of Manufactures

Notes: D = data suppressed; number included in the preceding category.

*Number does not equal 100% due to rounding errors.

| Gleason Works | Textron, Inc. |
| Acme-Cleveland Corporation | Ex-Cell-O |

Since 1900 the Midwest has been the leading machine tool producing area in the country, as noted in the previous chapter. Table 3 illustrates the geographic distribution of machine tool establishments for selected years from 1958–1982. As during the first half of the twentieth century, the majority of machine tool establishments have been located in the Midwestern States of Ohio, Indiana, Illinois, Michigan, and Wisconsin, an area designated by the Bureau of the Census as the East North Central Division. The fact that the center of the automobile industry has been in Detroit mainly explains the large number of machine tool firms located in the Midwest, and in particular, in the states of Michigan and Illinois. But many machine tool establishments have located in California also. For instance, in 1972, 1977, and 1982, Michigan has been the home of most machine tool establishments, followed by Illinois and then closely by California. While the automobile industry has contributed to the large number of machine tool establishments locating in the Midwest, the aerospace industry has no doubt done the same in California.

To summarize the more descriptive characteristics of the machine tool industry, it should be noted that, first of all, it is a relatively small industry. A second important feature of much of the machine tool industry is family ownership and control. Economic concentration is also a very salient characteristic of the machine tool industry, with the larger firms doing most of the business and employing the majority of workers. In regard to the geographic location of the machine tool industry, it is evident that the Midwestern States have been the home of many machine tool establishments, though the number in California has likewise been numerous.

AN ANALYSIS OF THE ECONOMIC CONDITIONS OF THE U.S. MACHINE TOOL INDUSTRY

As the preceding chapter pointed out, the business cycle has been extremely problematic for the U.S. machine tool industry for some time. Though the issue of demand will not be examined

Table 3. Geographic Location of Machine Tool Establishments by Divisions, 1958–1982

Year	New England	Middle Atlantic	East North Central	Other
1958	122	176	453	167
1963	150	251	545	221
1967	149	239	578	287
1972	140	218	620	300
1977(a)	155	197	595	254
1982(a)	147	132	587	158

Sources: Data from 1958-1972 from National Machine Tool Builders'
Association, 1978-1979 Economic Handbook of the Machine
Tool Industry (hereafter, NMTBA, 1978-1979 Handbook), p. 61;
and data from 1977 and 1982 from National Machine Tool Builders'
Association, 1984-1985 Economic Handbook of the Machine Tool
Industry (hereafter, NMTBA, 1984-1985 Handbook), p. 64.

(a) For 1977 and 1982, regional data does not equal the total in Table 1
because of a new methodoology used by the Bureau of the Census which
withholds data from some states.

Table 4. Net Income before Taxes as a Percentage of Sales for All Manufacturers and Machine Tool Companies, 1967–1983

Year	All Manufacturers	Machine Tool Companies*
1967	8.3%	12.1%
1968	8.8	11.6
1969	8.4	8.9
1970	6.8	3.8
1971	7.0	-2.7
1972	7.4	-1.3
1973	8.0	4.3
1974	7.7	5.6
1975	6.7	8.9
1976	7.8	9.3
1977	7.8	7.6
1978	7.8	7.4
1979	7.5	12.0
1980	6.7	12.9
1981	7.4	12.2
1982	5.3	5.0
1983	6.3	-9.6

Source: NMTBA, 1984-1985 Handbook, p. 257.

*Data for machine tool companies is from approximately 100 surveyed
companies.

in this chapter, but rather in the following one, it is nonetheless imperative to understand that the continuance and intensification of the effects of the business cycle on the U.S. machine tool industry have contributed to additional problems since the Second World War, especially in recent years. Because of the many problems stemming from the business cycle, the postwar years have witnessed the weakening of the American machine tool industry. The overall strength of the U.S. machine tool industry has also been diminished to some extent by the failure of the government to provide assistance for research and development to tool builders for civilian purposes. Coinciding with the weakening of the U.S. machine tool industry has been the growth and development of its foreign competitors. The machine tool industries of Japan and West Germany, most especially, have benefited at the expense of their American rival. It is to an analysis of the U.S. machine tool industry's additional problems that we now turn. The additional problems of the machine tool industry to be examined are the following: (a) sales and profits; (b) capital investments for new plant and equipment; (c) research and development; (d) low productivity; (e) backlogs and lead times; (f) shortages of skilled workers; and (g) imports and exports.

Sales and Profits

Because many machine tool companies are still privately owned, there is a dearth of public information available on the sales and profits of individual firms. Yet the NMTBA, from data collected for it by a research group, makes clear that net profits as a percentage of sales for machine tool companies have had the tendency to be slightly higher than that of all manufacturing industries during boom times and substantially lower during bust periods.[8] This actually is no surprise since machine tool business activity has very closely corresponded with the business cycle, and so expectedly sales and profits have been quite variable.

From Table 4 it is evident that economic contractions have hurt the business of machine tool companies. From 1967 to 1969 the statistic net income as a percentage of total sales for machine tool companies was higher each year than it was for all manufacturing industries. But owing to the recessions of 1969–1970 and 1973–1975, this statistic was lower for machine tool companies than it was for all manufacturers in every year from 1970 to 1974. By 1979 business for the machine tool industry was booming, and this trend continued into the first half of 1980. Although the 1981–1982 recession was bad for manufacturing industries, it was crippling to machine tool builders.

Expenditures for New Plant and Equipment

A direct and at the same time alarming result of the fluctuating sales and profits record of machine tool companies has been low expenditures for new plant and equipment. Since the machine tool industry's relationship to the business cycle is at times extremely negative most companies have been reluctant to invest in new plant and equipment. Yet a very notable increase in these expenditures for the machine tool industry did occur during some of the years of the Vietnam War. With sales and profits relatively healthy during the early years of the war, machine tool companies apparently were less reluctant to spend on new plant and equipment. But by 1970 capital investments within the machine tool industry began to sharply decline. Even when business has been exceptionally good, new capital investments have been relatively low. In both 1979 and 1980 expenditures for new plant and equipment in inflation-adjusted dollars were lower than they were in 1965. Low expenditures for new plant and equipment has meant that the U.S. machine tool industry has become less productive and less internationally competitive.

In 1978, the NMTBA conducted a study of sixteen large metalworking companies (covering the period 1960–1977). Along with generally declining capital spending on plant and equipment after 1970, the NMTBA study pointed to an even more disturbing fact. After adjusting for inflation, the book value of the fixed assets of these sixteen companies had deteriorated between 1970 and 1977 when compared to the 1965–1970 period. Quite correctly the NMBTA has recognized that the American metalworking industry has been involved in an "unconscious" and "involuntary" process of self-liquidation since 1970.[9]

Chart 1 indicates this marked deterioration for the machine tool industry as a whole. The recessions of the 1970s intensified the downward trend of the machine tool industry's fixed assets. However, since the 1973–1975 recession, the machine tool industry has been experiencing an even more threatening degeneration of its assets.

Research and Development

One of the most damaging problems of the U.S. machine tool industry for some time now has been low expenditures for research and development (R&D). A study on the machine tool industry completed by the Army in November of 1978 has very clearly indicated this problem. The Army's study pointed out that forty-three surveyed companies had devoted an average of 1.5% of their sales to R&D.[10] A later study published in 1983 reported a very similar figure for R&D.[11] If this figure can be taken as an indicator of the extent of R&D going on in most of the machine tool industry, then it is evident that the computer, automobile, office equipment, electronics, and the aerospace industries, to cite some examples, spend more on R&D.[12]

So despite the fundamental importance of machine tools to an advanced society like the U.S., the tool building industry has gone beyond frugality in regard to spending for R&D. Moreover, the machine tool industry generally has done little innovative or basic research. This means that a good deal of the new and advanced machine tool developments have originated outside of the industry, as will be shown in more detail below. Most of the R&D performed by machine tool builders has been mainly directed toward helping and assisting customers overcome problems encountered in production. As one big machine tool builder put it: "Research and development must be close to the customer and his problems rather than in a research laboratory."[13] Such customer application costs may tend to exaggerate R&D expenditures within the machine tool industry.[14]

Like capital spending on new plant and equipment, expenditures for R&D have been adversely affected by fluctuating sales and profits. This means that the business cycle has been the primary reason why most machine tool builders have themselves

Chart 1. Gross Book Value of Depreciable Assets of the Machine Tool Industry, 1962–1981

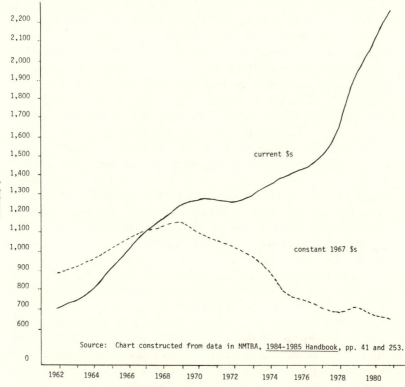

Millions $

current $s

constant 1967 $s

Source: Chart constructed from data in NMTBA, 1984-1985 Handbook, pp. 41 and 253.

1962 1964 1966 1968 1970 1972 1974 1976 1978 1980

neglected R&D expenditures. When the business cycle has turned downward, profits have fallen for machine tool builders. During periods of low profits, R&D spending has been among the first expenses cut back by tool builders. Noted one individual employed on the staff of the NMTBA when asked about R&D spending during slow business periods: "R&D is one of the first things to cut. People keep what they have to keep. R&D they don't have to keep."[15] This was evident during the 1981–1982 recession. Machine tool R&D expenditures in 1982 were just about the same, in inflation-adjusted dollars, as they were in 1975.[16] When the business cycle has turned upward, on the other hand, many machine tool builders have still been reluctant to substantially increase their R&D expenditures. But the reason for the reluctance of many tool builders to increase R&D spending has been different during good times. Improved business for the machine tool industry has meant growing backlogs (an issue to be more fully discussed below). The point is that during upturns in the business cycle, machine tool builders have tended to worry more about reducing their backlogs than about developing new products.[17] The major reason for this has been because, at least up until recently, when backlogs have increased, imports have also grown. Efforts to reduce backlogs, therefore, which has meant diverting capital away from R&D (for example, by increasing employment), has in large part been intended to curtail the import threat.

But it should be clearly understood that although the machine tool industry as a whole has by no means spent profusely on R&D, a few of the larger builders have not totally neglected these expenditures. For example, the biggest U.S. machine tool company, Cincinnati Milacron, spent 2.8% of its sales on R&D in 1977. This was higher than what all of the major automobile manufacturers spent on R&D as a percentage of their sales in this same year, except for Ford, and slightly above General Electric.[18] The top official at Cincinnati Milacron, James Geier, seems to have best expressed the firm's attitude toward R&D: "The name of the game is staying No. 1 in technology,."[19] Staying on top has indeed been Cincinnati Milacron's game plan. By 1982 Cincinnati Milacron could boast of its tenth consecutive annual increase in R&D expenditures.[20] In 1983 the company reported

R&D expenditures as a percentage of sales to be 5.4%. Another machine tool company, Brown and Sharpe, reported R&D outlays as a percentage of sales in 1983 to be 3.7%. Other big machine tool companies—Gleason Works (2.8%), Cross & Trecker (2.7%), and Acme-Cleveland (2.0%)—devoted a smaller percentage of their R&D expenses to sales in 1983.[21]

Nevertheless, the point is that most machine tool companies have not spent enough on R&D over the years and the major reason for this rather pervasive deficiency has been the business cycle. If the business cycle was not so greatly injurious to the machine tool industry, then more firms would undoubtedly have devoted additional expenditures to R&D.

In addition to the untoward effects the business cycle has had on most of the machine tool industry's R&D resources, another matter has also been very important. Most of the U.S. government's R&D expenditures during the postwar years have gone for military and related purposes. In other words, machine tool builders have not received technical assistance for civilian purposes from the government. So together, the injurious effects of the business cycle and government R&D funds mainly for military purposes have been damaging to the machine tool industry's ability to effectively compete with foreign builders, especially those in West Germany and Japan. Though U.S. builders had been the technical leaders in machine tool development since well before the beginning of the twentieth century, few would deny that their position has been steadily eroding in the last ten to fifteen years,[22] due to the increased metalworking R&D efforts abroad. Almost two decades ago a top official of a major international purchaser of machine tools, Ford Motor Company, noted that European builders have technically improved their equipment and that they have increased their machine tool R&D spending.[23] And a study performed by the University of Michigan in the mid–1960s, which then indicated potential metalworking progress for Japanese builders, pointed to the fact that Japanese universities and institutes were doing more machine tool R&D than was being done in the U.S.[24] Perhaps this issue was most felicitously expressed by James Gray, president of the NMTBA, who remarked in September of 1979 that "In Europe and Japan, research and development is a way of life for the machine tool industry. R&D funds come off the top. They are not a residual expense, to be invested *if* the money is available. As a result, our foreign competitors have generally narrowed the quality, productivity and technology gap."[25] Also, to some extent owing to the general paucity of machine tool innovations amongst American builders, some U.S. users have been researching and developing their own tools. (This particular matter will be dealt with in more detail in the concluding chapter.)

The deterioration of the technical superiority of the U.S. machine tool industry can be vividly seen by observing the change in the location of patents for metalworking machinery and equipment. A total of 84% of all patents for metalworking machinery and equipment in 1963 originated in the U.S.; one decade later U.S. patents had declined to 68%. Total U.S. patents for metalworking machinery and equipment were 2,642 in 1965; U.S. patents by 1973 had fallen to 1,976, or just slightly more than what they were in 1963. In short, foreign builders have made significant advances in regard to machine tool technology and development.[26]

The important question that now needs to be addressed pertains to how foreign builders, and particularly those in West Germany and Japan, have managed to become increasingly effective in their metalworking R&D efforts *in spite of business cycle effects on them*. The really big factor has been that financially their governments have been very supportive of and cooperative with civilian industries in the area of R&D. This is the exact opposite from what has been occurring in the U.S., where the presence of a technologically sophisticated military apparatus has created cooperation between the government and leading defense producers.

For some time now, there has been a rather close working relationship between tool builders and universities in West Germany, with funds coming about equally from both government and industry. Established in 1972, the government's Ministry of Research and Technology, along with the Economics Ministry, provide R&D funds to private industry. Government R&D funds have to be paid back (with little or no interest due) only if the product is a success on the market. However, if a tool builder develops a successful product with government money, he may be required to share his state-financed research with other builders. Beneficial also to the R&D efforts of the West German machine tool industry have been tax incentives from the government.[27] The central location for machine tool R&D in West Germany is the Machine Tool Laboratory of Aachen Technical University. This laboratory has a reputation for first researching a number of areas connected with machine tool developments. Other universities have also been active in metalworking research in West Germany, and they too have contributed to developments in machine tools. Remarked the Machine Tool Laboratory's chief in 1971: "Earlier, we always looked to America because new developments came out very quickly. Today, we're occasionally quicker. If we're looking for inspiration, we'd just as soon go to Japan."[28]

Large R&D expenditures for machine tool developments in Japan beginning by at least the middle of the 1960s eventually led to more sophisticated tool construction. Prior to roughly 1970 Japanese builders concentrated on exporting general or universal tools to the U.S. But along with increasing R&D expenditures for machine tool development, the Japanese began to place more emphasis on the production and marketing of advanced equipment, such as metalcutting numerical control machines.[29] Japanese production of numerically controlled machines increased from 1,369 units built in 1971 to 5,436 constructed in 1977.[30] By 1983 Japanese builders produced a total of 26,398 metalcutting numerical control machine tools. Of this amount, 4,076 (15%) were exported to the U.S.; by contrast the Japanese imported nineteen American numerical control machine tools.[31]

As in West Germany, the government of Japan has cooperated with machine tool builders by economically enlarging their R&D efforts. Loans for high-risk and new technologies from the Japan Development Bank and from the Research Development Corporation of Japan have been available to industries in Japan. Funds utilized on an unsuccessful product do not have to be repaid to the Research Development Corporation of Japan, whereas the developer of a successful product has five years to repay the no-interest loan to the corporation. Japanese tool builders have also benefited from tax incentives which promote new technologies in the private sector. Playing a major part in the maturation of the machine tool industry in Japan has been the Ministry of International Trade and Industry.[32]

In regard to actual technological allocations by nations, the early postwar differences in the directions of U.S., West German, and Japanese R&D expenditures are very apparent. An average of almost 60% of all R&D expenditures in the U.S. during the period 1959–1965 went for military and related purposes. West Germany during this same period expended only 9% of its total R&D funds on military and related work, while some 91% went for civilian purposes. Nearly all Japan's R&D expenditures in 1963 went for civilian purposes.[33] Clearly, as the U.S. was performing relatively large amounts of military R&D work, the countries of Japan and West Germany were upgrading the competitiveness of their civilian sectors, including the advancement of their machine tool industries.

Table 5 shows the percentage distribution of government R&D expenditures for West Germany, Japan, and the U.S. for selected years during the period 1963–1975. There is no doubt from Table 5 that the government R&D priorities of West Germany and Japan have been very different from those of the U.S. Very notable indeed is that the governments of Japan and West Germany, quite unlike the state in the U.S., have spent a significant amount of their R&D expenditures on the advancement of science and R&D as well as on other efforts in their civilian sectors. Also of interest is that in 1975 government-financed R&D for industrial growth totaled .5% in the U.S.; in Japan and West Germany, this figure was 6.5% and 7.4% respectively. By 1977 government-financed military R&D in the U.S. amounted to .658% of gross domestic product (GDP); by contrast in this same year government-supported defense R&D totaled .134% of GDP in West Germany and (probably) around .011% in Japan. Significantly, in 1979 the U.S. spent 81 dollars per capita on defense and space R&D, compared to 15 dollars per capita in West Germany and 3 dollars per capita in Japan. In this same year, out of twenty-two countries, the U.S. ranked amongst the lowest in per capita R&D funding by government in the two categories advancement of knowledge and agriculture and industry.[34]

The ramifications of the direction of America's postwar R&D

Table 5. Percentage Distribution of the Government R&D Expenditures of the U.S., West Germany, and Japan, 1963–1975

Year	Defense & Related	Advancement of Science & R&D	Other
U.S.			
1963/1964	83.3%	1.5%	15.2%
1970/1971	72.6	2.4	25.0
1975	63.6	3.9	32.9
West Germany			
1963	22.7%	37.0%	40.3%
1971	20.9	45.6	33.5
1975	11.1*	51.0	37.8
Japan			
1963/1964	2.2%	59.7%	38.1%
1969/1970	2.9	61.4	35.7
1975	2.2*	55.8	42.5

Sources: Organization for Economic Co-operation and Development, Patterns of Resources Devoted to Research and Experimental Development in the OECD Area, 1963-1971 (Paris: OECD, 1975) p. 42; and Organization for Economic Co-operation and Development, Technical Change and Economic Policy (Paris: OECD, 1980), p. 37.

Note: * = Defense only. While West Germany and Japan actively perform space R & D, much of this work is more likely to be for nonmilitary purposes, particularly in Japan. In the U.S., space R & D work is for military purposes.

expenditures have harmed the U.S. machine tool industry. To what extent the performance of massive amounts of military R&D has weakened the technological competence of the U.S. machine tool industry is difficult to say exactly. But it is clear that R&D funds directed toward the military and away from the civilian sector have proven beneficial to the U.S. machine tool industry's principal foreign competitors—Japan and West Germany—whose governments have directly applied technological expenditures to nonmilitary purposes. The fact that Japanese products accounted for almost 45% of U.S. machine tool imports in 1983 is strongly related to the government of Japan's very enthusiastic commitment to civilian technological progress over the years and its very minimal allotment of R&D expenditures for defense. Massive expenditures by the U.S. government for the advancement of science and R&D, had they occurred, could have only been advantageous to the machine tool industry. In one way this is clearly so since U.S. governmental expenditures directed toward the civilian sector would have created additional funds for the machine tool industry, given the adverse effects of the business cycle on its R&D resources.

It seems true nonetheless that R&D spending for military purposes contributed to the U.S. machine tool industry's technological lead over its foreign competitors, though the existence of this edge is presently a debatable issue. The first important postwar contribution the military made to machine tool technology was the underwriting of the costs of numerical control (NC) tools. NC tools brought increased automation and versatility to the machine tool industry. The NMTBA has termed NC machine tools as doubtlessly "the most important breakthrough of the century in metalworking technology."[35] But it must be pointed out that without financing from the Air Force, NC machine tools would certainly have had a delayed appearance.

The first major move toward the development of NC machine tools came in 1949 when the Parsons Corporation, a small firm manufacturing helicopter blades, acquired a $250,000 developmental contract from the Air Force. The president of the company believed that a technique previously experimented by the firm's research director could be further developed into an automatic control during the course of this Air Force contract.

Parsons Corporation subcontracted most of the work to the Seromechanisms Laboratory at the Massachusetts Institute of Technology (MIT) which during the Second World War had labored with a similar problem—developing automatic gunnery controls. Taking over as the Air Force's prime contractor, the Seromechanisms Laboratory by 1952 fully developed the first NC tool, a vertical milling machine, despite and subsequent to the contempt shown by nearly all tool builders. Both the Air Force and MIT, until 1953, vigorously attempted to interest U.S. machine tool builders and the aircraft industry in the incipient NC technology. However, only one U.S. tool builder, Giddings and Lewis, Inc., was interested enough to invest its money in NC equipment. From 1949 to 1959 the Air Force spent at least $62 million on the NC project. So the Air Force, along with the heavily defense-subsidized aerospace industry, was responsible to a large extent for the continued development of NC tools during the 1950s, and for the machine tool industry's eventual acceptance of this technology.[36] In short, the machine tool industry had little to do with the early development of NC equipment. But after the machine tool industry accepted NC tools, the production of this equipment by tool builders became fairly common (as it is presently).

The aerospace industry has continued to be a very large consumer of NC machines since their inception. Stemming from NC equipment was the development of even more advanced machines called computerized numerical control (CNC) and direct numerical control (DNC). Aerospace companies have also been major users of this advanced equipment. Aerospace companies performed much of the early developmental work on CNC and DNC machinery.[37] The rather extensive usage of and continued developmental work on NC and more recently CNC and DNC machinery by much of the aerospace industry should be juxtaposed with the fact that it has occupied a very paramount position during the post war years in the military-industrial complex. It likewise should be noted that both the aerospace industry and the military for a number of years have had a great interest in furthering machine tool technology.[38]

While CNC machines are commonly found in the aerospace industry, DNC tools, which are more advanced, are appearing with increased frequency. One of the country's largest users of DNC tools is McDonnell Douglas; in the late 1970s it had plans to expand its use of these machines.[39] It is decisive to point out here that McDonnell Douglas has been the recipient of many large military contracts. Another recipient of many and large military contracts, General Dynamics, has found DNC equipment to be more efficient than other tools. This is evident since General Dynamics included in its program to modernize its plant for the building of the F–16 Fighter a plan to install a new DNC machine shop.[40] The close relationship between the aerospace industry, the military, and advanced machine tool equipment can perhaps best be understood by noting what happened to Rockwell International at its Los Angeles division after the cancellation of the B–1 Bomber during the Carter administration. Not only did the cancellation of the B–1 Bomber idle a very large amount of NC equipment, but it also aborted Rockwell's plans to expand its CNC to DNC machinery.[41]

Other industries of course have made use of NC, CNC, and DNC machinery. But as the NMTBA has remarked, "the most spectacular use of numerical control is in the aerospace industry where it creates shapes unattainable by any other method."[42] Accordingly, this holds true for both CNC and DNC tools since they are actually the new generation of NC machining systems. Thus, like NC equipment, there is very good reason to believe that military spending has been at least a partial impetus to the continued advancement of both CNC and DNC machine tool technology[43] through the heavily defense-subsidized aerospace industry.

Though not an aerospace company per se, a very complex DNC machine has been developed by General Electric's Aircraft Engine Group and the Army Manufacturing Methods and Technology Program. This development further demonstrates the military's interest in advancing metalworking technology, the need for more sophisticated machinery in aeronautical construction, and innovation occurring outside of the machine tool industry. Only one U.S. machine tool company was willing when the project began to participate in it. However, the machine the U.S. firm developed proved to be inadequate. Machine tool companies apparently believed the project involved high risks and they were content with what they considered to be enough low-risk work. Very significant also is the fact that one Army official commented that this machining system is "quite simply the most modern machining system of its type in the world."[44]

A few more advanced machining processes also evince the military's interest in them and their development other than by machine tool builders. These advanced processes are high-speed, ultrasonic, and hot or laser machining. Experimentation on high-speed machining first began at Lockheed Aircraft Corporation in the 1950s. Underwriting the costs of this research beginning in the 1950s was the Department of Defense. This process has had a relatively long developmental period, and even today it is not a widely used machining technique. Nonetheless, tests on high-speed machining and military funding for them have continued at Lockheed. And Lockheed has used high-speed machining on parts for the Trident Missile.[45]

Support by the Department of Defense has likewise been essential in the development of ultrasonic machining. Most of the recent R&D funds for the development of this relatively new and embryonic machining process has been provided by the Army Aviation Research and Development Command to a subsidiary of the Hughes Helicopter Company. The continued development of this machining process will be very beneficial to the aerospace industry.[46]

It seems that all three of the military services have developed an interest in hot machining, and especially in laser machining. Whether the military's interest will grow to the point where it will fully underwrite the costs of the research needed to improve laser machining is not clear. But it is evident that the machine tool industry has not been the innovator of this advanced and quite expensive machining process. Rather, one of the leading innovators in this area has been the Center for Laser Studies at the University of California.[47]

Other advanced metalworking techniques suggest development outside of the machine tool industry, along with the possibility of at least some financial support from the military. Such nontraditional machining processes as electrical discharge machining, electrochemical machining, and high energy rate forming have been most widely used in the aerospace industry. Once again it is important to recall that most machine tool companies have not done much advanced research and few even have laboratories for such work. So the use of these machining processes in the aerospace industry, which itself has done a large amount of innovative and military R&D, is a noteworthy fact.[48] Moreover, much metalworking R&D has been performed in various laboratories, institutes, and universities,[49] and they too have received financial support from the Department of Defense.

In this analysis of machine tool R&D and technology, three points are particularly important: (1) the machine tool industry has not spent too much money on R&D; rather, these expenditures have been relatively low; (2) initially a good many advanced metalworking developments, and frequently continuous improvements made on this equipment, have come from outside of the machine tool industry; though this is not to say that the machine tool industry itself does not produce advanced equipment; and (3) the aerospace industry has been a major user of advanced metalworking equipment and it also has continuously received large defense subsidies, however other industries, such as the automobile, have made good use of both advanced machine tools and machining processes. This third point very strongly suggests that machine tool technology has been advanced to some extent as a result of the symbiotic relationship between the military and the aerospace industry. Furthermore, the fact that universities, research institutes, and laboratories have also been involved in machine tool R&D work while at the same time receiving many defense dollars, points even more to the military's role in advancing metalworking technology.

Owing to all of these facts, there should be little doubt that the technological sophistication of many U.S. machine tools has been the result, in large part, of excessive R&D spending for military purposes. But it is just as important to understand that the erosion of the machine tool industry's technological lead has likewise resulted mainly from exorbitant R&D spending for the military. Thus the technical sophistication of U.S. machine tools, resulting to some extent from military expenditures, has at the same time helped to create the conditions which have reduced, or possibly eliminated, this technological edge over the foreign competition. Much of America's postwar R&D spending has been substantially different from these expenditures in West Germany and Japan, as noted above. Excessive spending on R&D for defense in the U.S., while certainly advancing machine tool technology, has not had the same effects on civilian metalworking technology relative to societies where R&D expenditures have been overwhelmingly for nonmilitary purposes. Had U.S. postwar R&D spending taken a path similar to the one taken by West Germany and Japan, there would be a very good reason to believe that American tool builders would not be experiencing a shrinking technological lead. This argument is asserted despite both the harmful effects of the business cycle on the industry and the tax R&D incentives found in both Japan and West Germany.

In summary, the technological problem in the U.S. machine tool industry has stemmed from two major factors. The first has been the adverse ramifications the business cycle has had on the R&D resources of the machine tool industry. The second factor, and somewhat of a corollary of the first, has been that at least partially due to the general lack of innovation amongst tool builders, a good deal of advanced R&D work has taken place outside of the machine tool industry. This last point should be viewed in the light of the fact that U.S. expenditures on military R&D during most of the postwar years have been extremely high, which certainly has contributed to making much of the advanced technological work done on metalworking equipment outside of the machine tool industry geared first toward meeting defensive and related ends. Extremely large R&D expenditures for defense, moreover, have preempted funds that could have been enormously helpful to machine tool builders. Thus the combined effects of the government's strong emphasis on defense expenditures after the Second World War and the machine tool industry's inability and reluctance to spend sufficiently on R&D have certainly been major reasons for its technological predicament, that is, given the increasing sophistication of the products of Japanese and West German builders.

Productivity in the U.S. Machine Tool Industry

Productivity within the machine tool industry has been low for four major and interconnected reasons: (1) both sales and profits have fluctuated with the business cycle; (2) this, in turn, has reduced significantly the amount of capital available for investment in new plant and equipment; (3) an inadequate supply of skilled workers; and (4) an insufficient amount of technical innovation. The first three reasons are straightforward. With permanent shortages of skilled workers and without sufficient sales and profits to generate adequate investment capital for new plant and equipment, productivity will be negatively affected. In regard to the last reason, since the U.S. machine tool industry has not been technologically innovative, due in large part to the business cycle and also because of the inability of builders to procure civilian R&D funds from the government, improvements (such as new, more productive equipment) needed to increase output have been neglected. Thus, taken together, these four reasons, along with the fact that capital from exports has not acted as a compensatory factor against the business cycle, explain the productivity problem of the U.S. machine tool industry.

It is generally known that productivity increases in recent years in the U.S. have been small relative to most advanced capitalist societies. Probably not as well known is the fact that productivity in the U.S. machine tool industry has been worse than in the American manufacturing sector as a whole. For example, productivity during the period 1967–1977 in manufacturing increased an average of 2.41% a year; for the U.S. machine tool industry during the 1967–1976 period productivity actually declined an average of .96% a year.[50] Similarly, during the period 1973–1981 manufacturing productivity in the U.S grew by an average of 1.7%; in the machine tool industry the average yearly decline was .7%.[51] Having a very damaging impact on U.S. machine tool productivity is that the percentage of machine tools twenty years old and older within the machine tool industry itself increased steadily from 1973 to 1983. By 1983 more than 45% (up from 35% in 1973) of the machine tools in use in the machine tool industry were twenty years old or older.[52]

Productivity in the machine tool industry has been especially poor during economic slowdowns. Productivity in the machine tool industry during the 1969–1970 recession dropped by 13.9% in 1970. The following year it dropped again, this time by 6.8%.

In the 1973–1975 recession productivity fell by .9% in 1974 and by 9.1% in 1975. In short, during periods of slow business activity, because sales and profits have declined reducing capital available for investment in new plant, equipment, and R&D, and since the skilled work force has shrunk, productivity has taken a turn for the worse.

The poor productivity of the U.S. machine tool industry was instrumental in removing American builders from their once dominant position as the world's leading producers during much of the 1970s. U.S. machine tool production as a percentage of total world output started declining in 1968. In the middle of 1971, West German builders surpassed U.S. output and became the world's foremost machine tool producers until the late 1970s. In 1979, U.S. builders regained the lead for a while, but by 1982 the Japanese led all competitors in the production of machine tools. (See Chart 2.) Significantly, an International Trade Commission study found that Japanese machine tool productivity has grown to twice the size of what it is in the U.S.[53]

Poor productivity in the U.S. machine tool industry has contributed immensely to its generally higher-priced products. That is, since total output has not been sufficient to offset the rising labor and other costs of U.S. builders, prices have continuously been increasing for American-made machine tools; this has meant that users of metalworking equipment in this country have turned more and more frequently to lower-priced foreign goods, which recently have been even more attractive because of the high value of the dollar relative to other foreign currencies. Another result of the high prices of American machine tools is that U.S. users have not been quickly replacing their old metalworking equipment.[54] In the two metalworking surveys conducted by the *American Machinist* (AM) in the 1970s, the U.S. had the lowest percentage of machine tools under ten years old of a number of industrial countries. During both of these surveys the U.S. also had the highest percentage of machine tools over twenty years of age.[55]

Table 6 indicates that U.S. users of machine tools are still more reluctant to purchase new equipment than users in other industrial nations. Of the seven countries listed in Table 6, the

Table 6. Age of Machine Tools in Seven Industrial Countries

Country	Year	% under 10 yrs. old	% over 20 yrs. old
United States	1983	32.4	33.1
Canada	1978	35.8	33.8
West Germany	1980	34.0	48.0 d
France	1980	35.0	32.0
Italy	1975	38.0 a	28.0 e
Japan	1981	36.4 b	35.6 f
Great Britain	1982	42.3 c	27.2

Source: Calculated from "The 13th American Machinist Inventory of
           Metalworking Equipment 1983," American Machinist, November
           1983, pp. 116 and 118.

a -- o to 8 years old
b -- 0 to 7 years old
c -- 0 to 5 years old
d -- 15 years and older
e -- 18 years and older
f -- 13 years and older

Chart 2. Percentage of World Production for the U.S., Japan, and West Germany, 1964–1983

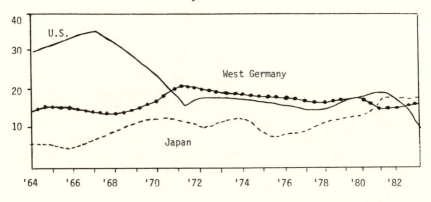

Sources: NMTBA, 1978-1979 Handbook, p. 150; and NMTBA, 1984-1985 Handbook,
            p. 162.

U.S. has the smallest percentage of machine tools under ten years old. Given the different age categories for older machine tools presented in Table 6, it is difficult to determine exactly how U.S. aged equipment compares to that in other countries.* However, from the previous AM survey, published in late 1978, to the most recent one, the percentage of American machine tools over twenty years of age has only minimally declined; for machine tools under ten years old, the percentage has increased slightly, but is still below the figures reported in 1973, 1968, and 1963.

It is therefore noteworthy to indicate that, due to the high prices of American machine tools and despite the import invasion, much obsolete machinery has remained in the plants of users of metalworking equipment throughout the country. Obsolete machine tools have had a very direct and consequential impact on productivity in the U.S. Since new machine tools are essential in order to improve output, and given the age of U.S. metalworking equipment compared to that of other advanced capitalist societies, one should not find it surprising that productivity in America has been poor relative to many other industrial nations. Most notable of all of the major industrial nations has been Japan. In Japan manufacturing productivity over the last twenty years has been significantly greater than in the U.S. During the 1973–1983 period the average annual increase in manufacturing productivity in Japan was about 6.8%, while in the U.S. it was under 2%. In Japan in 1973, some 60% of its machine tools were under ten years old; in 1981 over 36% of Japan's machine tools were under eight years of age.

One final point should be mentioned here. The relatively large amount of antiquated metalworking equipment in the U.S. over the years has had far-reaching effects on the economy of this country. Besides the nation's productivity problem, obsolete machine tools have aggravated inflation, most notably in the past. (This entire issue will be fully elaborated on in the final chapter.)

---

*As of 1983, out of seven industrial nations, the U.S. had the highest percentage of tools in the age group 10–19 years. See NMTBA, *1984–1985 Handbook*, p. 261.

Backlogs and Lead Times

Due largely to the effects of the business cycle, the machine tool industry has been subjected to shifting backlogs. Backlogs have increased and have been extremely high when the economy has been strong and prosperous. When the economy has slowed down, the backlogs, or unfilled orders, of machine tool companies have declined, though by no means have they ever been small. A brief historical review of the backlogs of the machine tool industry indicates very clearly their cyclical nature. In 1956, unfilled orders totaled $990 million. The following year, and the beginning of the 1957–1958 recession, backlogs fell to $471 million, only to decline still more in 1958 by another $163 million. With the recession over in 1959 the unfilled orders of the machine tool industry began to climb. Backlogs were extremely high during the years 1964 to 1969, that is, during the midst of the war in Vietnam. But another recession caused backlogs to decline by over 50% from 1969 to 1971. Backlogs began to grow in 1972 and continued to do so until 1975 when, by this time, America's sixth postwar recession pushed unfilled orders for machine tools down once again. After the recession, as usual, backlogs started to increase again, and in 1980 they reached a postwar high of $5.541 billion. The very severe recession of 1981–1982 produced a precipitous decline in backlogs. In December of 1983 backlogs were the lowest they had been in over ten years.[56]

There is no doubt that the president of the NMTBA, James Gray, was looking only at the optimistic side of the backlog issue when he commented on the huge volume of unfilled orders the industry had accumulated by the end of 1978. According to Gray, the large quantity of unfilled orders at the end of 1978 boded "well for the future prospects of the U.S. machine tool industry since it was an indicator of the strength of future shipments."[57] In the past the growth of backlogs when business has been good not only has indicated prospective shipments, but has also helped to cushion, though only a little, the machine tool industry from the relatively bad times it has faced during periods of contracted demand. The issue of backlogs, however, has also had a disadvantageous side to it. And most definitely these disadvantages have outweighed the advantages.

Partly owing to the specialized nature of some machine tools but mostly because of the large backlogs that have resulted during boom periods, lead times (the period from when new orders are placed until production is actually completed on them) have been too extensive. Also contributing to long lead times in the machine tool industry have been small capital expenditures, low productivity and R&D spending, and a chronic shortage of skilled workers (the last of these will be discussed below). By the late 1970s, lead times in the machine tool industry were over one year for many tools. In December of 1980, while backlogs were $5.451 billion, shipments for the year totaled $4.692 billion. This meant that unfilled orders had a higher dollar value than that of total shipments in 1980, or more than one year's worth of work had accumulated in back logs.

But lead times have for quite some time been long in the machine tool industry. Table 7 shows the ratio of backlogs to total shipments for each year from 1956–1983. These ratios are not exact indicators of lead times; however, they do serve as rough estimates. Though a major cyclical decline in backlogs occurred in 1982 and 1983, this will prove to be temporary, and consequently, lead times will not change significantly in the long run.

There have essentially been two major and interrelated problems connected with long lead times. The first problem has been the rising prices of machine tools. Long lead times coupled with high postwar inflation have meant added costs incurred by builders from the time when orders have been placed until work has been completed on the equipment. To safeguard against unnecessary profit reductions, builders have passed on their rising costs to their customers. It has become imperative for machine tool builders to pass on their increased costs to their customers because of poor productivity within the metalworking industry. Many builders have tried to protect themselves from rising costs by either not quoting a price to the buyer until the tool has been built or by using price-escalation clauses in their contracts.[58] However, the 1981–1982 recession did have a dampening effect on machine tool prices. For example, between 1979 and 1980 machine tool prices grew by almost 17%, but between 1982 and 1983 they rose by only 2.6%.[59]

Table 7. Ratio of Backlogs to Total Shipments of Machine Tools, 1956–1983

Year		Year		Year	
1956	.72	1965	.92	1974	1.29
1957	.38	1966	1.01	1975	.59
1958	.52	1967	.73	1976	.77
1959	.72	1968	.62	1977	1.01
1960	.60	1969	.75	1978	1.21
1961	.62	1970	.49	1979	1.39
1962	.56	1971	.57	1980	1.16
1963	.70	1972	.94	1981	.65
1964	.90	1973	1.38	1982	.33
				1983	.57

Source: Calculated from NMTBA, 1984-1985 Handbook, pp. 77 and 79.

Note: A ratio of 1 equals one year.

Table 8. Inventories of the U.S. Machine Tool Industry, 1958–1981

Year	Work in Progress	Finished Products	Material & Supplies
1958	49.6%	27.5%	22.9%
1963	53.1	26.4	20.4
1967	59.5	21.4	19.1
1969	59.3	20.7	20.0
1970	55.8	24.1	20.1
1972	54.5	23.9	21.5
1974	59.0	19.5	21.6
1976	56.9	22.3	20.8
1978	60.6	19.7	19.7
1980	65.1	18.9	16.0
1981	61.9	23.2	15.4

Sources: Calculated from NMTBA, 1978-1979 Handbook, p. 69; and NMTBA, 1984-1985 Handbook, p. 72.

The second problem closely related to long lead times has been foreign competition. Because the prices of U.S. machine tools have been rising continuously, foreign products have increasingly become much more attractive to American buyers, especially in the last fifteen years. As the ex-president of the NMTBA, Tim Perkins, put it in 1976: "We have to be very careful about prices. We can't get out of line price-wise, or we'll lose to foreign competition."[60] Unfortunately, U.S. builders have been losing out to the foreign competition (as we will see in more detail below). Queried members of the NMTBA seem to be in agreement with the fact that many foreign machines have been purchased for less in the U.S. than similar American products. And a top executive of one of the bigger machine tool companies, Giddings & Lewis, Inc., when asked the question if it was true that many foreign machine tools have sold for less in the U.S. than comparable products made in this country, responded by saying, "Yes, from what we've been told."[61] A recent study of the machine tool industry maintained that Japanese firms have been selling some tools in the U.S. from 10 to 40% lower than those produced by American builders.[62]

The truth of the matter is that, unlike the U.S. machine tool industry, some foreign builders, and particularly those in West Germany and Japan, have managed to reduce their lead times through the utilization of very automated production techniques.[63] Mainly because of this—and also partly due to the fact that while for the most part increasing their output, foreign machine tool workers, especially in Japan and Great Britain, have been compensated less than their U.S. counterparts—overseas builders have generally been able to sell their products for lower prices. The shortened lead times of foreign builders which simultaneously helps to reduce backlogs, moreover, has partially contributed to prompt deliveries for them. For the U.S machine tool industry, conversely, long lead times have meant even longer delivery times. According to the International Trade Commission's study on the machine tool industry mentioned previously, it is generally true that American builders utilize longer lead times than their major foreign competitors.[64]

Besides the lengthy lead times characteristic of the U.S. machine tool industry, another reason for long delivery times has been that overall finished products have not been preponderant in the inventories of American builders, as Table 8 indicates. Indeed, the vast majority of the inventories of the machine tool industry during the years shown in Table 8 have been made up of work in progress. On the other hand, only about 20 to 25% of the inventories of the machine tool industry have been comprised of finished products. With a relatively small amount of finished machine tools in stock and with large backlogs which have generally made lead times extensive on many tools, delivery times for American products have become increasingly less competitive with those of foreign builders. This has been true first of all since some foreign builders, as noted, have reduced their lead times. Second, many foreign builders have been forced to stock standard tools. Without stocking standard tools and because of lengthy shipping times, foreign builders would find it very difficult to compete with the few large U.S. firms that stock *some* standard machines or with those companies who could build this equipment from parts on hand in a short period of time. By maintaining most of the standard machine tools desired by their customers in their inventories, foreign builders have been able to quote short delivery times on this stocked equipment.[65] For these two reasons then, foreign builders have been able to have shorter delivery times than U.S. producers on most machine tools. In a comment said to typify the attitude of American machine tool producers, one builder asserted the following: "Long delivery times are causing problems in connection with our competition form overseas, particularly Japan. Most of our foreign competition is talking about immediate deliveries, or deliveries in 60 days."[66] While Japanese builders could deliver machine tools to American manufacturers in the late 1970s within a month or two, some U.S. builders were taking between a year and a half and two years.[67]

A good example of the shorter delivery time and also the lower price of foreign tools is the Japanese numerical control (NC) machining center. The NC machining center is a computerized and very versatile tool capable of performing a number of different operations which previously required many machines. Japanese NC machining centers have become quite popular in the U.S. because they are less expensive than similar American-made tools. But the popularity of Japanese NC machining centers has also been enhanced due to short delivery times. Delivery times for American built NC machining centers have been twelve to eighteen months, while Japanese builders have delivered these tools in three months.[68]

Additionally, machine tool users have emphasized the greater reliability of equipment built by Japanese producers and the very careful attention to service rendered by them after sales.[69] Several Japanese builders have maintained that they can guarantee service on their products within forty-eight hours.[70] This is important to metalworking users. Prompt service on equipment reduces the "down time" of machinery. Minimizing the "down time" of machine tools means that production will only be interrupted for a short period of time and that profits will not be significantly reduced due to the continuation of most costs and the slowing down of output. U.S. metalworking users increasingly then are likely to view Japanese machine tools as practical buys in the future since, along with their other attractions, the guarantee of quick service made by some Japanese builders is advantageous to industrial efficiency from the perspective of business.

Thus in regard to prices, lead and delivery times, and even reliability and service the U.S. machine tool industry has been finding it more and more difficult to compete with foreign builders. Had civilian R&D expenditures been made available by the government to machine tool builders, then the probable introduction of very automated production techniques similar to those utilized by Japanese and West German producers could have helped to reduce lead times, while also diminishing backlogs. But since this type of government assistance has not been available, nor is it imminent, one of the few things U.S. builders can do to compete is to make sure that the products they deliver impress their customers.[71]

Employment and Skilled Workers

Employment in the U.S. machine tool industry has been highly contingent on the state of the economy. A healthy and prospering economy has meant increased employment, while a flagging one has had the effect of reducing the number of workers in tool building companies. Because employment has significantly decreased at times, as can be seen from Chart 3, there has resulted a chronic shortage of skilled workers in the machine tool industry. Even during exceptionally good times the machine tool industry has had to contend with a shortage of skilled workers.[72]

It generally takes several years before skilled workers employed by machine tool companies are fully trained at their jobs. Due to this lengthy training period skilled workers cannot easily be replaced, at least not within a short time. So when employment has been cut back by machine tool companies as a result of economic downturns, many skilled workers who also lost their jobs have turned elsewhere for work. Skilled workers have sought work elsewhere because they have very much wanted to avoid future unemployment—something which is rather difficult in the extremely cyclical machine tool industry. Thus because machine tool companies have layed off skilled laborers during slow periods and since many of these workers have sought and apparently acquired different jobs, there has resulted a perennial shortage of highly qualified productive personnel. The fact that there has been a shortage of skilled workers has also contributed to the U.S. machine tool industry's operating below full capacity when business has been good.

Between 1981 and 1982, as a result of recession, employment in the machine tool industry declined by 20%. Employment in the industry has been estimated to be even lower in 1983, reaching its lowest point since this data was first compiled for both metalcutting and metalforming employees. At the same time, the machine tool industry operated at less than 40% of capacity, despite the improvement in new orders.[73]

While employment has also been curtailed by West German and Japanese builders during slow periods, it seems that the scarcity of skilled workers has hurt the U.S. machine tool industry more. This is so since the Japanese and the West German machine tool industries have demonstrated increased competitiveness in the world market at the expense of U.S. producers. So despite fluctuating employment in the West German and Japanese machine tool industries, the fact remains that since

Chart 3. Total Employment in the U.S. Machine Tool Industry, 1958–1983

Thousands

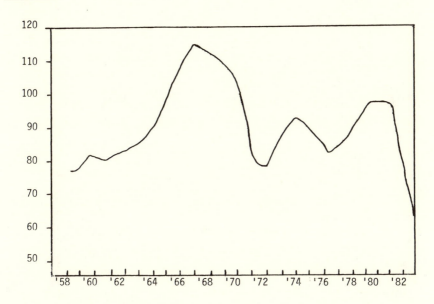

Source: NMTBA, 1984-1985 Handbook, p. 234.

Note: Figure for 1983 is an estimate.

Chart 4. U.S. Exports and Imports of Machine Tools and Parts, 1958–1983

Millions of Dollars

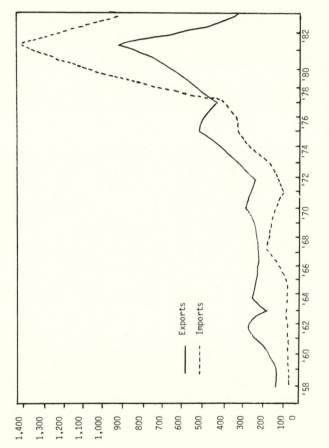

Source: Data on machine tool exports and imports from NMTBA, 1984–1985 Handbook, p. 126.

their civilian-oriented and state-supported R&D programs have increased their international competitiveness, the loss of skilled workers has not been as problematic for these foreign industries. In contrast, the lack of civilian R&D subsidies to U.S. builders incorporated in a state-supported industrial policy has contributed in large part to their becoming less competitive in the world market, and this means that export demand has not been able to reduce the large number of skilled workers who have been layed off during periods of slow domestic business.

Imports and Exports

A combination of factors have been responsible for the U.S. machine tool industry's critical import problem. Foremost among these factors has been the small R&D expenditures of most U.S. tool builders coupled with huge technological outlays by the state for military purposes. Other major and notable factors contributing to the import problems of the U.S. machine tool industry have been low capital expenditures for new plant and equipment, shortages of skilled personnel, higher-priced American tools, long lead and delivery times, large backlogs, and low productivity. When taken together, these factors indicate that the effects of the business cycle and a military-distorted R&D effort in the postwar years have been very harmful to the U.S. machine tool industry since the result has been a continued influx of foreign products into the American market—one of the biggest machine tool consuming markets in the world.[74] As can be seen from Chart 4, imports of machine tools and parts have been growing almost steadily from the late 1950s. While exports have also grown, Chart 4 shows very clearly that imports have increased even faster, finally resulting in a deficit in machine tools in 1978.

The first big onslaught of machine tool imports began in about the middle of the 1960s, coinciding with the war in Vietnam. Imports during these years were mainly general purpose and standard tools. From around 1970 onward, American users of metalworking equipment also began to import more sophisticated machine tools.[75] The upshot of this was that imports to the U.S. soon began increasing at an unprecedented rate. The severity of the import invasion became very apparent to machine tool builders by the time of the 1973–1975 recession. In the past imports have tended to follow backlogs very closely; when backlogs grew so did imports, and when backlogs fell imports declined. But when backlogs fell during the recession of 1973–1975, for the first time imports continued to spiral upward.[76]

Though there was not an overall trade deficit until 1978, metalcutting tools fell into the red in 1977, and certain tools even before that. A trade deficit in boring machines, including vertical turret lathes, began in 1966, for example. Drilling machines, milling machines, and lathes, not including vertical turret lathes, have gone through periodic trade deficits. Thus the penetration of foreign machine tools into the U.S. market was a gradual process which, by at least 1977, became an alarmingly disproportionate problem for U.S. tool builders.

American machine tool imports over the years have come mainly from five countries—West Germany, Japan, Great Britain, Italy, and Switzerland, though in recent years imports from Taiwan have become very important. (See Table 9.) For many years, West German machine tool imports dominated the U.S. market. Beginning in 1977, Japanese machine tools became the biggest import threat. By the end of 1983, as Table 9 indicates, nearly 45% of all U.S. machine tool imports came from Japan.

Assisted by their government in their R&D effort, Japanese tool builders in the mid–1960s began to understand the importance of gaining a sizeable share of the U.S. market. And clearly, as noted above, Japanese builders have recognized and responded to the expanding market in the U.S. for advanced machine tools. Significant also is that Japanese producers have started to set up subsidiaries in the U.S.,[77] in the absence of which imports from Japan would be even larger.

West German machine tool builders by the late 1960s, even before Japanese producers, began establishing subsidiaries in the U.S.[78] In spite of this, West German imports have been in demand for some time in the U.S., even though they have recently lost much ground to Japanese products. In recent years, Japanese and West German products have constituted almost 60% of U.S. machine tool imports.

The statistic imports as a percentage of machine tool con-

Table 9. U.S. Imports of Complete Machine Tools from Selected Countries, 1965–1983

Year	West Germany	Japan	Great Britain	Switzerland	Italy	Taiwan
1965	34.5%	8.5%	13.7%	15.8%	9.4%	(a)
1966	30.0	14.7	14.6	12.8	10.0	(a)
1967	28.5	14.7	18.5	8.7	12.5	(a)
1968	31.5	12.0	17.8	9.8	10.5	(a)
1969	30.2	11.5	15.6	8.6	13.1	(a)
1970	35.4	11.2	15.6	8.9	7.8	(a)
1971	34.2	10.9	12.6	11.6	8.5	.1
1972	34.4	12.9	13.2	10.4	6.7	.2
1973	30.9	13.2	13.1	12.0	6.0	.5
1974	28.8	17.5	11.4	10.8	6.2	.9
1975	30.2	19.7	12.4	8.5	4.9	.8
1976	29.3	21.1	10.0	9.0	4.6	4.1
1977	22.8	26.4	11.5	8.8	3.8	5.6
1978	21.6	30.8	10.5	8.0	3.6	6.8
1979	18.9	33.8	9.3	6.3	3.6	8.2
1980	18.2	37.9	9.0	6.3	3.4	7.2
1981	13.0	46.4	9.2	5.3	2.9	6.9
1982	16.3	42.2	8.6	5.7	3.6	7.2
1983	13.3	43.8	7.0	5.8	5.2	8.8

Sources: Table constructed from data found in NMTBA, 1978-1979 Handbook. p, 147; and NMTBA,1984-1985, Handbook, p. 128.

(a) Relatively insignificant.

Table 10. Imports as a Percentage of Domestic Machine Tool Consumption for the U.S., Japan, and West Germany for Selected Years, 1960–1983

Year	U.S.	Japan	West Germany
1960	5.4%	31.1%	19.6%
1965	4.5	17.7	17.8
1970	9.5	13.6	23.8
1975	14.5	14.2	27.8
1978	21.5	8.2	29.9
1979	23.3	9.2	29.8
1980	23.6	8.5	32.8
1981	25.6	6.6	28.4
1982	27.7	8.0	25.4
1983	34.2	7.0	24.7

Sources: NMTBA, 1978-1979 Handbook, p. 164; and NMTBA, 1984-1985 Handbook, p. 184.

Chart 5. Share of World Exports, 1969–1983

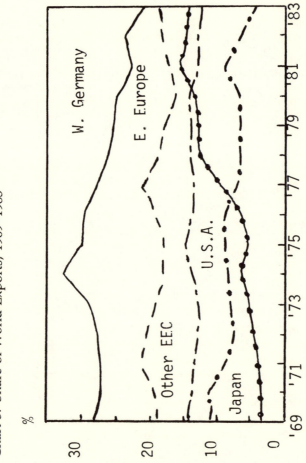

W. Germany

E. Europe

Other EEC

U.S.A.

Japan

%

30

20

10

0

'69 '71 '73 '75 '77 '79 '81 '83

Source: NMTBA, 1984–1985 Handbook, p. 167.

sumption in the U.S. has increased by more than six times from 1960 to 1983, as indicated in Table 10. The figures for Japan show that imports have become a less important factor in its domestic market, since this percentage has declined substantially during the period 1960–1983. Table 10 shows that West Germany noticeably increased its consumption of foreign products for a while, though lately a decline is evident. But West Germany's imports have been offset by their large volume of exports.

Healthy trade surpluses in machine tools have been quite common in West Germany. More than any other machine tool industry, the West German tool building industry has been tied very closely to the world market. West German machine tool builders exported over 58% of their total production in 1983; the figures for Japanese and U.S. builders were 35.4% and 16.8% respectively. West German tool builders' exporting practices have resulted in their taking the lion's share of the world export market for some time, as Chart 5 makes clear.

The critical turning point for Japanese machine tool builders came in 1972. That year marked the beginning of sizeable and sustained trade surpluses for the Japanese. After 1972 the Japanese machine tool industry's share of world exports began to noticeably increase. Japanese products continued to penetrate the global export market and by 1977 their share of world exports surpassed that of the U.S.

A recent problem slowing down the growth of U.S. exports of machine tools has been the American government's imposition of restrictions concerning trade with socialist countries who have increasingly become major consumers of metalworking equipment. But the major effects of this problem only really began to be felt in 1976. (See Chapter 5.) U.S. exports of machine tools have not been at any American producer's optimal level for some time. Clearly the conjunction of steadily rising prices for U.S. machine tools, long delivery times, and the availability of high-quality and high-technology tools from foreign builders have made world users of metalworking equipment less willing to purchase American products.

Since 1964 the U.S. share of the global export market has been declining. From about 21% in 1964, the U.S. machine tool industry by 1983 had less than 5% of the world export market.

Maintaining the share of the global export market held in 1964, along with fewer foreign imports, would have been beneficial to both the sales and profits of U.S. builders, and consequently, more capital would have been available for investment in R&D and in new plant and equipment. Very problematic for American builders has been that domestic recessions, which have reduced business at home, have become even more disastrous for them owing to their declining share of world exports. In this respect, the president of the NMTBA, James Gray, remarked that: "By losing a substantial portion of the global machine tool market, we have been exacerbating our industry's roller-coaster business cycle because we have become increasingly dependent upon a smaller portion of the market and consequently more sensitive to the fluctuations in the American business cycle."[79]

West Germany has not been without recessions in the postwar years. The big difference between the West German and the U.S. machine tool industries is that the former has maintained a relatively large share of the world export market for a number of years, whereas the latter's portion has become less and less significant. This means that recessions that have occurred in West Germany have not had the same damaging effects on its machine tool industry as economic slowdowns have had on U.S. builders. Because the Japanese share of the world export market has been increasing for the most part since the early 1970s, this has helped to cushion the impact of the worldwide recessions of 1973–1975 and 1981–1982 on tool builders in Japan. With more emphasis being placed on exports in Japan, future recessions will be less detrimental to its machine tool industry.

It has generally been agreed upon by most analysts of the U.S. machine tool industry that the growth of imports and the concomitant loss of a significant share of the world export market has been the direct result of the increased competence and the determined competitiveness of the West German and, especially in recent years, Japanese tool builders. The question that now needs to be answered is how have the West German and Japanese tool builders managed to be so successful in their competitory efforts at the expense of U.S. producers. As in the U.S., most of the tool producing companies in West Germany and Japan are not large. Most Japanese and West German machine tool companies employ fewer than thirty workers each.[80] Though total compensation to workers in machine tool companies has been significantly less in Japan than in the U.S., together the wages and benefits of West German employees have not been much lower than those of American laborers in metalworking firms.[81] In this respect, since total compensation to West German metalworking employees has not been too different from that given to U.S. workers and because most machine tool firms in both Japan and West Germany, very much like those in this country, are not large companies, these facts provide no really effective grounds for explaining the import-export predicament of American builders. However, one major answer proffered has been the greater government assistance for R&D found in Japan and West Germany, and in many other countries also, which, in turn, has benefited foreign machine tool industries. What has not been suggested nor even alluded to by analysts of the U.S. machine tool industry has been that the R&D expenditures of the West German and Japanese governments have been overwhelmingly civilian-oriented, while in America this most definitely has not been true during most of the postwar years.

Thus it is not that the U.S. government has been remiss in regard to assisting private enterprise in its R&D progress, for one need only to look to the aerospace industry, for example, in order to dispute this argument. Rather, the nucleus of the issue pertains to the type of governmental R&D assistance that has existed in excess in the U.S. during most of the postwar years. Exorbitant R&D expenditures for defense and related purposes in the U.S., compounded by the damaging impact of the business cycle on tool builders, have indisputably given the machine tool industries of West Germany and Japan the opportunity to increase their civilian technological competence. Along with the fact that they have taken full advantage of this opportunity, West German and, more recently, Japanese tool builders have tied themselves to the global market, and with prices which have been more appealing to users of metalworking equipment.

CONCLUSION

This chapter has analyzed the basic structural characteristics of the U.S. machine tool industry, apart from demand. The machine tool industry is a very important (important, that is, to the industrial health and vitality of the U.S.) capital-goods industry. This chapter has argued that this capital-goods industry has been weakened as West German and Japanese machine tool builders have become stronger.

Owing to the machine tool industry's very close economic relationship to the business cycle, it has had to contend not only with fluctuating demand, but also with the additional problems discussed in this chapter. Besides the problems related to the business cycle, another factor has been underscored in parts of this chapter which also has contributed to a weakened machine tool industry. This was the large and persistent R&D expenditures for military purposes in the U.S. In short, the sustained high levels of military spending in the U.S. during most of the postwar years that has preempted massive R&D expenditures for defense, while in some respects advancing metalworking developments, in the long run has been a major impediment to the international competitiveness of the machine tool industry. This has been so since, unlike most U.S. builders who have been in desperate need of R&D funds because of the harmful effects of the business cycle on them, machine tool producers in West Germany and Japan have received support for their civilian technological efforts from their governments (as have foreign builders in some other capitalist countries).

NOTES

1. Data on the machine tool industry from the National Machine Tool Builders' Association, *1984–1985 Economic Handbook of the Machine Tool Industry* (hereafter NMTBA, *1984–1985 Handbook*), p. 253; figures for General Motors and Exxon from *Business Week* (Scoreboard Special Issue), March 21, 1984, pp. 70 and 78.

2. Standard & Poors, *Industry Surveys, Machinery*, May 27, 1976, p. M–19.

3. "Can U.S. Machine Tools Maintain an Edge?" *Industry Week*, August 21, 1978, p. 71.

4. "A Machine Maker with Optimism," *Business Week*, November 20, 1971, p. 46.

5. National Machine Tool Builders' Association, *Directory 1979.*

6. Date calculated from the National Machine Tool Builders' As-

sociation, *1978–1979 Economic Handbook of the Machine Tool Industry* (hereafter NMTBA, *1978–1979 Handbook*), pp. 66–67.

7. Calculated from the U.S. Bureau of the Census, *1972 Census of Manufactures*.

8. See NMTBA, *1984–1985 Handbook*, pp. 251, 256–57.

9. See "Statement by Craig R. Smith, Second Vice Chairman, National Machine Tool Builders' Association, for a Meeting with Secretary of Commerce Kreps on Capital Cost Recovery" (not dated; hereafter, NMTBA Statement to Secretary of Commerce Kreps on Capital Cost Recovery); and "Is Metalworking Manufacturing Committing Economic Suicide?" *Production Engineering*, August 1978, p. 41.

10. Hintz et al., *Machine Tool Industry Study: Final Report*, p. 36.

11. The National Research Council, started by the National Academy of Sciences, is responsible for this study. The findings of this study appear in the Committee on the Machine Tool Industry, Manufacturing Studies Board, Commission on Engineering and Technical Systems, National Research Council, *The U.S. Machine Tool Industry and the Defense Industrial Base* (Washington, D.C.: National Academy Press, 1983), pp. 14 and 49 (hereafter, Committee, *The U.S. Machine Tool Industry*).

12. See "Vanishing Innovation," *Business Week*, July 3, 1978, pp. 46–47; "A Deepening Commitment to R&D," *Business Week*, July 9, 1984, pp. 65–70.

13. See "Can U.S. Machine Tools Maintain an Edge?" *Industry Week*, August 21, 1978, p. 66.

14. Committee, *The U.S. Machine Tool Industry*, p. 14.

15. Interview with a spokesman from the NMTBA.

16. See Committee, *The U.S. Machine Tool Industry*, p. 15 for figures.

17. *Production Engineering*, August 1978, p. 42.

18. "Vanishing Innovation," *Business Week*, July 3, 1978, pp. 46–47. It is worth pointing out that Milacron is a diversified company. (See Chapter 4.) This means that not all of Milacron's R&D expenditures have been allotted to machine tool development. Moreover, and most importantly, Cincinnati Milacron is one of the country's leading producers of industrial robots, and the market for them has only just begun to open up. Thus it is very likely that much of Milacron's R&D funds in recent years have been devoted to improving its computerized robots. See "Robot Production Gain of 300% Target for Cincinnati Milacron," *American Metal Market*, February 5, 1979, p. 17.

19. See "A Machine Maker with Optimism," *Business Week*, p,. 46.

20. See *Moody's Handbook of Common Stock*, Fall 1984 ed. (New York: Moody's Investor Service, Inc., 1984).

21. All figures for 1983 from "A Deepening Commitment to R&D," *Business Week*, July 9, 1984, p. 73.

22. According to the Department of Commerce, "The U.S. machine tool industry over the past decade has experienced a gradual erosion of its technological lead." See U.S. Department of Commerce/Industry and Trade Administration, *1979 U.S. Industrial Outlook*, p. 236.

23. "American Machine Tools—A World Customer's View," *Automation*, December 1966, p. 44.

24. "Japan Tops in Metalworking R&D," *Iron Age*, October 21, 1965, p. 101.

25. Emphasis is Gray's. See Gray, "Machine Tool Exports: A Smaller Slice of a Bigger Pie," p. 10.

26. "Assessing Technology in Machine Tools," *American Machinist*, October 1975, p. 53.

27. See Committee, *The U.S. Machine Tool Industry*, pp. 115–16; Hintz et al., *Machine Tool Industry Study: Final Report*, pp. 43–44; and also NMTBA Statement, March 21, 1978.

28. Quoted in "Germany Edges into Tool Lead," *American Machinist*, March 8, 1971, p. 74.

29. See "Japanese Tool Makers Chart Market Course," *Iron Age*, March 18, 1971, p. 24.

30. NMTBA, *1978–1979 Handbook*, p. 178.

31. NMTBA, *1984–1985 Handbook*, p. 198.

32. On the R&D incentives available in Japan, see Holloman, "Technology in the United States: Issues for the 1970's," p. 16; NMTBA Statement, March 21, 1978; and also Committee, *The U.S. Machine Tool Industry*, pp. 111–13.

33. These figures are from Hollomon and Harger, 'America's Technological Dilemma," p. 37. While Hollomon and Harger's figures indicate that all of Japan's 1963 R&D expenditures went for civilian purposes, apparently the Japanese government did spend a very small amount on military R&D in this year. (See Table 5.)

34. See Organization for Economic Co-operation and Development, *Technical Change and Economic Policy*, pp. 37 and 40. The 1977 figure for Japan is an estimate based on the 1975 figure. All government per capita figures and information from Organization for Economic Co-operation and Development, *OECD Science and Technology Indicators* (Paris, OECD, 1984), pp. 34–35.

35. National Machine Tool Builders' Association (booklet), *Machine Tools/New Concepts for a New Day*.

36. See "How to Talk to Machine Tools," *Fortune*, March 1962, p. 124; "Making a Machine Run Itself," *Business Week*, March 9, 1957, pp. 183–87; "Can U.S. Machine Tools Maintain an Edge?" *Industry Week*, August 21, 1978, p. 68; and David F. Noble, "Social Choice in Machine

Design: The Case of Automatically Controlled Machine Tools," *Case Studies on the Labor Process*, ed., Andrew Zimbalist (New York: Monthly Review Press, 1979) pp. 18–50.

37. See "Computer Looms Large in N/C Picture," *Iron Age*, August 15, 1968, p. 26; "When Computers Run the Machines," *Iron Age*, September 19, 1968, pp. 87–94; "Computers Take on More Jobs," *American Machinist*, November 18, 1968, pp. 117–18; and "Advanced Metalworking Concepts Used in Production," *Automation*, December 1968, pp. 15–16.

38. For example, the Aerospace Industries Association's Ad Hoc Manufacturing Equipment Panel "was set up to help federal agencies determine long-range needs for defense manufacturing programs." Quoted in the *American Machinist*, May 23, 1966, p. 39. Though a very intense relationship similar to the one apparent during World War II between the machine tool industry and the defense sector has not existed for some time, nevertheless there have been a number of military groups established for the purpose of advancing machine tool technology. One such more recent group was the 100-member Machine Tool Task Force organized by the Air Force. One of the findings of a 1983 study of the U.S. machine tool industry indicated that the interest of the Department of Defense in this industry "includes having access to state-of-the-art technology. . . ." Committee, *The U.S. Machine Tool Industry*, p. 3.

The Department of Defense's Manufacturing Technology (Man-Tech) program—instituted in the 1950s—is meant to facilitate the practical application of new manufacturing processes. The Army, through its Man-Tech program, has been involved in an effort to provide more information on FMS (flexible manufacturing systems, a process in which a single computer integrates and controls the functions of a group of machine tools) to manufacturers who are not fully informed about this new technology. Several U.S. machine tool builders have been involved in this effort with the Army. See Ibid., pp. 19, 56–59.

39. See "McDonnell Douglas Expands DNC Machining," *American Metal Market*, March 12, 1979, p. 12.

40. See "Modern Plant Cuts F–16 Output Costs," *American Metal Market*, July 3, 1978, p. 10.

41. See "Rockwell N/C Equipment Idled, DNC Plan Aborted," *American Metal Market*, April 10, 1978 (supplement), p. 14a.

42. National Machine Tool Builders' Association (booklet), *Machine Tools/New Concepts for a New Day*.

43. In regard to funding by the Air Force of DNC, see Noble, "Social Choice in Machine Tool Design: The Case of Automatically Controlled Machine Tools," p. 40.

44. However, a Swiss tool building company developed a machine that was suitable for the project. See "GE Program Challenges U.S. Machine Tool Innovativeness," *Iron Age*, August 27, 1979, pp. 101–02.

45. On high-speed machining see "Ultra-High-Speed Machining," *American Machinist*, February 22, 1960, pp. 111–26; "High Speed Machining," *American Machinist*, March 1979, pp. 115–30; and "Missile Parts Machined at Ultra-High Speeds," *American Metal Market*, May 29, 1978, p. 10.

46. See "Ultrasonic Machining Studied to Speed Production," *American Metal Market*, April 30, 1979, pp. 10 and 14.

47. See "Hot Machining Called Superalloy Cutting Key," *American Metal Market*, August 21, 1978, p. 8.

48. The aerospace and missiles industry has been a leading industrial R&D spender. However, the vast majority of its R&D effort over the years has been for defense and related purposes. Government money going to this industry for defense and related R&D constituted 87% of its total R&D expenditures in 1963, 77% in 1968, and 74% in 1975. Calculated from the National Science Foundation, *Research and Development in Industry 1975* (Washington, D.C.: U.S. Government Printing Office, 1977). This has not changed in the 1980s. In 1981 federal R&D funds going to the aerospace industry, most of which were for defense and related purposes, were estimated to make up 80% of this industry's total R&D expenditures. The estimated figure for 1982 was 74%. Calculated from Aerospace Industries Association of America, Inc., *Aerospace Facts and Figures, 1982/83* (New York: Aviation Week & Space Technology, 1982), p. 106.

49. See James G. Abert and Clayton McCuistion, *The Defense Dependency of the Metalworking Machinery and Equipment Industry and Disarmament Implications*, p. 169.

50. The figure for the average change in productivity for manufacturing industries during the period 1967–1977 and the one for the machine tool industry during the 1967–1976 period are from Hintz et al., *Machine Tool Industry Study: Final Report*, p. 16.

51. These figures are from Committee, *The U.S. Machine Tool Industry*, p. 17.

52. See NMTBA, *1984–1985 Handbook*, p. 261.

53. See "US Machine Tools vs. Foreign Competition," *American Machinist*, November 1983, p. 23.

54. Cf. Seymour Melman, *The Permanent War Economy*, pp. 81–82.

55. See "The 11th American Machinist Inventory of Metalworking Equipment 1973," *American Machinist*, October 29, 1973, p. 149; and "The 12th American Machinist Inventory of Metalworking Equipment 1976–1978," *American Machinist*, December 1978, p. 135.

56. Data from NMTBA, *1984–1985 Handbook*, p. 79.

57. Quoted in "Will '78's Machine Tool Boom Heard in '79?" *Iron Age*, January 15, 1979, p. 39.

58. "The Profitless Boom in Machine Tools," *Business Week*, July 6, 1974, p. 52.

59. Since 1950 the producer price index for machine tools has risen steadily. However, in 1974 the producer price index for machine tools began to increase at a very rapid pace, and it did not really slow down until the 1981–1982 recession took its toll on the industry. The following is a list of the annual percentage changes in the producer price index for machine tools from 1970–1983.

Year		Year		Year	
1970	6.5%	1975	17.3%	1980	16.8%
1971	3.6	1976	8.9	1981	10.8
1972	3.0	1977	8.5	1982	7.2
1973	6.5	1978	11.8	1983	2.6
1974	18.8	1979	14.5		

Data for the producer price index for machine tools from NMBTA, *1984–1985 Handbook*, p. 41.

60. Quoted in "Inflation to Wind Down for Machine Tool Buyers," *Purchasing*, November 9, 1976, p. 10A11.

61. Responses are from questionnaires sent to the National Machine Tool Builders' Association and to Giddings and Lewis, Inc.

62. Committee, *The U.S. Machine Tool Industry*, p. 29.

63. Hintz et al., *Machine Tool Industry Study: Final Report*, p. 20.

64. See "US Machine Tool Industry vs. Foreign Competition," *American Machinist*, November 1983, p. 23.

65. Hintz et al., *Machine Tool Industry Study: Final Report*, pp. 19–20.

66. Quoted in "Will '78's Machine Tool Boom Be Heard in '79?" *Iron Age*, January 15, 1979, p. 40.

67. See Committee, *The U.S. Machine Tool Industry*, p. 27. However, the delivery time for some tools has been more than three years. See Hintz, et al., *Machine Tool Industry Study: Final Report*, p. 20. Interesting here is the comment made in June of 1980 by James Geier, then president and chief executive officer of Cincinnati Milacron, the country's largest machine tool company: "Our machine tools sell for about $2 million *each* and deliveries now extend well into 1982." See *The Wall Street Transcript*, June 23, 1980.

68. "No Impact Yet from 'Check Price' System," *American Metal Market*, July 17, 1978, p. 20.

69. See Committee, *The U.S. Machine Tool Industry*, p. 28. Another study reported better after-sales service on specialty tools by U.S. builders than their major foreign competitors and just the opposite for standard tools. See "US Machine Tools vs. Foreign Competition," *American Machinist*, November 1983, p. 23.

70. "Machine Tools Lose an Export Edge," *Business Week*, February 5, 1979, pp. 25–26.

71. Cf. "Aerospace Technology Keeps Steady Altitude," *Iron Age*, March 12, 1979, p. 38.

72. See NMTBA, *1984–1985 Handbook*, p. 233.

73. See U.S. Department of Commerce, *U.S. Industrial Outlook 1984*, p. 20–1.

74. In 1976 and 1977 U.S. consumption of machine tools was second only to the Soviet Union. See NMTBA, *1978–1979 Handbook*; p. 151. In 1981 and 1982 the U.S. was the leading machine tool consumer. See "World Machine-Tool Output Falls 20%," *American Machinist*, February 1983, p. 81. However, by 1983 the U.S. had fallen to third place behind Japan and the Soviet Union. See "Machine Tools Post a Slow Year," *American Machinist*, February 1984, p. 76.

75. In the beginning of 1971 the vice president of Warner & Swasey Company remarked: "Unfortunately foreign competition is beginning to move from the simpler pieces of equipment into the technologically sophisticated ones." Quoted in "Are Machine Tool Builders With It?" *Industry Week*, January 11, 1971, p. 40.

76. See NMTBA, *1978–1979 Handbook*, p. 127; and also "Imports— The Machine Tool Industry's Achilles' Heel," *Mechanical Engineering*, January 1978, p. 73.

77. See "$2-Million Earmarked by Yamaszki for Expansion of Kentucky Plant," *American Metal Market*, January 23, 1978, p. 10; and "Reaching Out—Japanese Control Makers Establish Links to Export Marts," *American Metal Market* (supplement), April 10, 1978, p. 48.

78. Machine Tool Competition Toughens Here and Abroad," *Iron Age*, August 27, 1979, p. 76.

79. Quoted in "Why World Trade Problems are Everybody's Problem— or Will Be Soon,"*Iron Age*, January, 1978, p. 69.

80. On the average number of workers in many West German machine tool firms see Hintz et al., *Machine Tool Industry Study: Final Report*, p. 33; and for Japan see "How Metalworking Grows in Japan," *American Machinist*, March 1977, p. 80.

81. See NMTBA, *1978–1979 Handbook*, p. 222; NMTBA, *1984–1985 Handbook*, p. 248.

4

Machine Tool Demand and Defense Spending

The important issues relating to machine tool demand will be analyzed in this chapter. Particular attention will be given to how machine tool demand has been affected by military spending. That military expenditures have been high and that they have fluctuated in the U.S. for most of the postwar period has been an important factor in determining machine tool demand. But this kind of relationship has not existed for machine tool builders in Japan and West Germany. The absence of this type of relationship has been advantageous to machine tool producers in these countries.

THE BUSINESS CYCLE AND MACHINE TOOL DEMAND

Probably more than any other industry, the machine tool industry has experienced feast or famine in regard to demand for its products. As emphasized in Chapter 2, fluctuating demand has been the most critical problem for the machine tool industry and for metalworking companies for many years. When the economy has been thriving the demand for machine tools has been strong. But when economic slowdowns have occurred the demand for machine tools has weakened. Notes the U.S. Department of Commerce: "The machine tool industry is a cyclical industry, strong when other industries are investing in plant and equipment to modernize, and weak when these same industries are experiencing a slump or are in a period of low profitability."[1] So for the machine tool industry, when the gross national product has contracted there have been drastic reduc-

Table 11. Annual Percentage Changes in Real Domestic New Orders of Machine Tools and the Real Gross National Product (GNP), 1958–1983

Year	Machine Tools	GNP	Year	Machine Tools	GNP
1958	—	—	1971	-1.6%	3.4%
1959	81.0%	6.0%	1972	61.9	5.7
1960	-20.4	2.2	1973	71.1	5.8
1961	-.4	2.6	1974	-18.9	-.6
1962	20.6	5.8	1975	-58.4	-1.2
1963	31.0	4.0	1976	69.2	5.4
1964	49.5	5.3	1977	27.2	5.5
1965	7.9	6.0	1978	30.2	5.0
1966	15.4	6.0	1979	7.4	2.8
1967	-36.3	2.7	1980	-25.2	-.3
1968	.5	4.6	1981	-45.4	2.6
1969	10.8	2.8	1982	-54.1	-1.9
1970	-54.7	-.2	1983	20.1	3.3

Sources: Data for machine tools calculated from NMTBA, 1984–1985 Handbook, p. 78; real GNP data from the Economic Report of the President Washington, D.C.: U.S. Government Printing Office, 1984), p. 223.

tions in the demand for its products. During the recession of 1957–1958, for example, the real (adjusted for inflation) gross national product declined by 1.1% and domestic new orders of machine tools fell by over 45%.[2] Because of the variability of new orders of machine tools, moreover, they have been labeled as the "barometer" and "the best measure" of the economic conditions of the capital-goods sector of the economy.[3]

Table 11 shows the annual percentage changes in real domestic new orders of machine tools (both metalcutting and metalforming types) and also those for the real gross national product during the period 1958–1983. Table 11 makes evident that during the postwar recessions of 1960–1961, 1969–1970, 1973–1975, 1980, and 1981–1982 domestic new orders of machine tools significantly decreased with deteriorating economic conditions. Evidence of the sensitivity of machine tool demand is also apparent during the period 1966–1967. From October of 1966 to June of 1967 the U.S. experienced what has been termed a "mild recession." Domestic new orders of machine tools in constant dollars declined between 1966–1967 by $724 million, or by 36%. In short, Table 11 only serves to substantiate what has already been said about machine tool demand. That demand has been greatly reduced during recessions and has been relatively healthy during good times is one unambiguous fact concerning the machine tool industry.

U.S. users of metalworking equipment have in the past typically purchased new machine tools for the following reasons: (1) to improve the quality of their products; (2) to develop new products; (3) to increase production; (4) to lower their operating costs; and (5) to replace old equipment.[4] But Chapter 3 indicated that machine tool users have not been replacing their old equipment as quickly as have users in many other advanced capitalist societies. Also indicated in Chapter 3 was that obsolete equipment has remained in many manufacturing plants in the U.S., despite even the large influx of imported machine tools, largely as a result of the relatively higher prices for American-made metalworking products.

Looking at domestic new orders of machine tools in constant (1967) dollars is revealing since this further suggests the general reluctance of machine tool users to replace their aged equipment

Chart 6. Domestic New Orders of Machine Tools in Current and Constant (1967) Dollars, 1956–1983

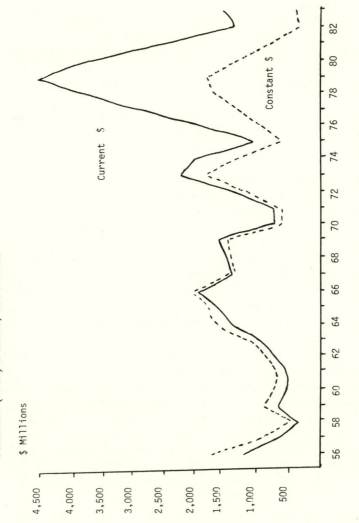

Source: Domestic new orders of machine tools in constant (1967) dollars calculated from NMTBA, 1984–1985 Handbook, pp. 41 and 78; domestic new orders in current dollars from ibid., p. 78.

with American-built products, while also illustrating the effect recessions have had on domestic demand. Even with substantial increases in domestic new orders when the economy has been unusually strong, purchases of machine tools in constant dollars have never gone beyond the point reached in 1966, as shown in Chart 6. This strongly suggests that a very big stimulant to domestic machine tool demand during the mid–1960s was the Vietnam War. The gradual dissolution of the war stimulant clearly had a detrimental impact on domestic metalworking demand, while it also "normalized" poor machine tool replacements by users. Equally apparent from Chart 6 is that in constant dollars there is a striking similarity in reduced machine tool demand during recessions. Thus when the economy has slowed down during postwar recessions U.S. metalworking users have been very willing to do without new machine tools—and to a similar degree in each recession.

MAJOR USERS OF MACHINE TOOLS

Most machine tools in the U.S. are located in the metalworking industries, which consist of the following: primary metals, fabricated metal products, electrical machinery, nonelectrical machinery, transportation equipment, precision instruments, metal furniture/fixtures, and miscellaneous manufacturing. Of the estimated 2,896,754 machine tools in the U.S., according to the 1983 metalworking survey by the *American Machinist*, some 2,192,754, or 76%, are in the above industries. Within these groups the biggest users of machine tools presently are, in order, the nonelectrical machinery, the fabricated metal products, and the transportation industries.[5]

A closer examination of these three major industrial categories yields more specific information concerning machine tool usage and consumption. Within each of these three industrial groups there are a number of individual industries. Table 12 lists the leading users of machine tools within these industrial categories. The largest consumer of machine tools is the metalworking machinery industry—which includes the machine tool industry. The metalworking machinery, the miscellaneous machinery, and the general industrial machinery industries are part of the larger

Table 12. The Top Six Industrial Consumers of Machine Tools

Industry	Units
Metalworking Machinery	201,995
Miscellaneous Machinery (except electrical)	199,401
Motor Vehicles	153,247
Fabricated Structural Metal Products	120,290
General Industrial Machinery	109,984
Aerospace	107,421

Source: Adapted from "The 13th American Machinist Inventory of Metalworking Equipment 1983," American Machinist, November 1983, pp. 117-18.

Table 13. Prime Military Contract Awards for Machine Tools, Fiscal Years 1974–1983

	(dollars in thousands)
Year	Dollar Amount
1974	38,070
1976	18,708
1980	215,147
1981	233,789
1982	32,083
1983	48,143

Sources: NMTBA, 1978-1979 Handbook, p. 111; and NMTBA 1984-1985 Handbook, p. 120.

classification nonelectrical machinery industry. Outside of the nonelectrical machinery industry, the motor vehicles, aerospace (both of which are part of the transportation industry), and the fabricated structural metal products industries are very big consumers of machine tools. In the metalworking inventory published in late 1978, the aerospace industry (consisting of both aircraft and parts and guided missiles and space vehicles) ranked fifth in machine tool consumption.

A large nonindustrial owner of machine tools is the federal government. In 1978 the federal government owned a little over 100,000 machine tools, with the Department of Defense in possession of the majority of them. In 1983 the Defense Department owned more than 63,000 machine tools.

MACHINE TOOL DEMAND AND MILITARY EXPENDITURES

Even though the Pentagon owns a sizeable number of machine tools, and despite the fact that military production requires large quantities of tools, during peacetime the Department of Defense nonetheless has not ordinarily procured much equipment *directly* from the machine tool industry, as shown in Table 13. Prime military contracts represented only 1.2% of domestic new orders for machine tools in 1977 and 3.1% in 1983. Even during the military "tooling up" period in 1981, defense contracts for machine tools amounted to only 9% of domestic new orders. For the most part, many of the machine tools necessary to sustain and improve the weaponry of America's colossal military apparatus have been purchased from the machine tool industry by large defense contractors.

Many of the major defense contractors are also big consumers of machine tools. For example, out of the top 100 prime military contractors in fiscal year 1978 nearly one-half were firms that consumed large quantities of machine tools. Specifically, many big defense contractors are part of the metalworking industries. Through much of the 1970s, out of the thirty-three companies that were at some time among the top twenty prime military contractors, twenty-eight were large metalworking-consuming firms.[6] In the 1980s the big defense contractors will need many machine tools to cut and form the metals used in the ongoing military buildup.

Focusing just on the top ten military contractors indicates more clearly the relationship between metalworking-consuming companies and defense production. Many of the big military contractors have been producers of aerospace equipment. For example, seven out of the ten leading military contractors in fiscal year 1978 were major aerospace producers. As already indicated, the aerospace industry has been one of the biggest consumers of machine tools. The remaining three companies (two of which were mainly electrical equipment producing firms and the other a conglomerate) were also large consumers of machine tools.[7] In fiscal year 1984 at least seven of the top ten defense prime contractors were major aerospace builders.

Chapter 2 made very clear how increased defense spending stimulated machine tool production during World War I and World War II. And defense production during the Korean War (1950–1953) utilized over a quarter of a million machine tools,[8] this amount is equivalent to at least 83% of the metalcutting machine tools shipped during the years 1950–1953. The war in Vietnam also contributed substantially to increased machine tool demand, as mentioned above. Though the exact total effects of military spending on machine tool demand cannot be determined for the Vietnam War period, it can be definitively shown that the Department of Defense's prime military contract awards for machine tools had a very big impact on metalworking demand during this war, especially in the early years of the conflict. In fiscal year 1965, prime military contract awards for machine tools totaled $39,943,000.[9] But in fiscal year 1966, as domestic new orders of machine tools began to approach a high point, prime military contracts for machine tools soared to $94,032,000. This represented an increase in prime military contracts for machine tools of 135%. In fiscal year 1967, which covered a full six months of calendar year 1966, prime military contract awards for machine tools were $72,340,000—still quite high. Prime military contracts increased to $78,171,000 in fiscal year 1968 before declining considerably in the latter part of the war. By also taking into consideration the indirect effects of defense spending on machine tool demand (for example, prime contractors who purchase metalworking tools for military production), it is clear that a very large number of machine tools were utilized in the production of military equipment during the Vietnam War. The following statement, made by the National Machine Tool Builders' Association, alludes to the big impact of military spending on machine tool demand during the Vietnam War: "In the Vietnam war. . . because of the specialized nature of the fighting . . . the need was for machine tools to produce jet fighter bombers, reconnaissance planes, helicopters, artillery shells, and small-diameter rockets and fuses."[10] Indeed, during the years 1962–1965, domestic new orders of machine tools averaged $1,103,175,000; but for the four-year period 1966–1969, during which time total prime military contract awards were for the most part exceptionally high, new orders averaged $1,498,675,000, over 35% more than in the previous period.[11]

But actual wars have not been the only military stimuli to machine tool demand. Permanently being prepared for war has also had a stimulating effect on the machine tool industry since 1950. The fact is that an important part of machine tool output has resulted because of military spending and production during the postwar years. Since the Korean War the machine tool industry no longer has had to completely "tool up" for military production. A war economy and ongoing defense production have become indelible features of the U.S. since the conflict in Korea and they have had important repercussions on the machine tool industry. It is significant to note in this respect the remarks of a U.S. Senate Committee: "Not one plane can be made, one ship launched, or one missile produced without hundreds and thousands of intricate machine tools."[12] A study prepared for the U.S. Arms Control and Disarmament Agency commented that the armaments industry is "a market for a relatively large share of the annual output of the machine tool industry, and although machine tools of every type are used by the government or by private contractors in producing military hardware, certain types are especially critical to military programs."[13] Apart from the more advanced technological equipment, some of the other machine tools used in military production are the following: milling machines, grinding machines, boring machines, automatic chucking machines, automatic screw machines, lathes, and vertical turret lathes.[14] Because of the large number and many different types of machine tools needed for armaments production in government plants and even more so in the establishments of military contractors, spending by the Department of Defense has clearly been an important stimulus of machine tool demand.

DEFENSE PROCUREMENT AND MACHINE TOOLS: 1950–1978

By virtue of the fact that military spending has contributed to stimulating machine tool demand during the postwar years, the logical corollary of this would seem to be that reductions in defense expenditures would have an opposite effect. In this respect it becomes important to examine the extent to which reduced military expenditures, which have occurred periodically during the postwar years, have contributed to weakening machine tool demand. Actually, what is really needed is a more detailed account of the long-term relationship between fluctuating military expenditures and machine tool demand. At this time the important question becomes: What is the relationship between fluctuating machine tool demand and postwar military expenditures?

It would seem that in order for military spending to have been not only an important but also a continuing component of metal-working demand, it would have had to closely correspond with the business cycle since this has been the fate of the machine tool industry. This is actually what has occurred from after World War II to the late 1970s. The significant and protracted effects military spending had in regard to both increasing and decreasing machine tool demand, after it declined drastically following World War II, began with the institution of the permanent war economy in 1950. Standard & Poors, in its 1954 industrial survey of metalworking machinery, after pointing to the reduced demand experienced by the machine tool industry as a result of the recession of 1948–1949, noted the following:

A reversal occurred in 1950, however, with the improvement in general business and the outbreak of warfare in Korea in June, 1950. Large pool orders placed by the General Services Administration for machine tools in connection with the defense program raised shipments sharply in 1951 and 1952, and to a nominal degree in 1953.[15]

Concerning the aftermath of the Korean War, this same report pointed out that reduced military procurement made inevitable a sizeable decline in total machine tool sales in 1954.[16] Adversely affecting machine tool sales also after the Korean War was the recession of 1953–1954. (Total metalcutting shipments dropped off by nearly $300 million in 1954 from the preceding year and by another $221.4 million in 1955.)

Chart 7 graphically depicts the continuing relationship between fluctuating, though always exorbitant, military contracts and variable domestic machine tool demand from 1956 to 1978. (The computation of the correlation coefficient for the twenty-three–year period shown on Chart 7 resulted in r = .8191). Not only did domestic orders of machine tools tend to increase when military contracts increased, but also the reduction in demand for metalworking equipment largely corresponded with reductions in defense spending. In other words, both military contracts and machine tool demand to a large extent were in keeping with the business cycle. More specifically, military-Keynesian policies affected domestic machine tool demand, both directly and indirectly, through fluctuating weapons procurement contracts which evidently had been used by the government to help regulate the business cycle. (This is not meant to say that fluctuating military contracts either caused or ended recessions, but rather that they had been used by the state to assist in the management of the business cycle.)

Thus it does appear that military spending noticeably contributed to both the good *and* bad times of the machine tool industry during much of the postwar years. Though increasing and decreasing war expenditures had definitely been related to metalworking demand prior to 1950, the continuance of a permanent war economy and military-Keynesian policies sustained the impact of the defense sector on the business activity of the machine tool industry. It should be understood also that when defense contracts were cut back, coupled with the general reluctance of metalworking users to replace their old equipment,

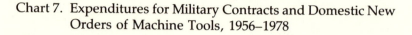

Chart 7. Expenditures for Military Contracts and Domestic New Orders of Machine Tools, 1956–1978

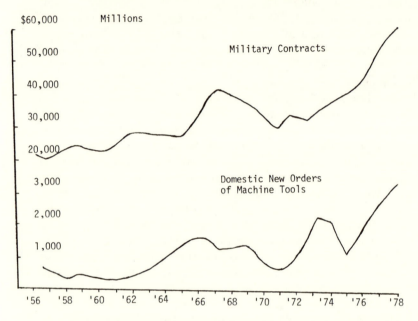

Sources: Data on military contracts for fiscal year 1956 from Business
Conditions Digest, December 1969, appendix, series 625; military
contracts for fiscal years 1957-1978 from the Department of Defense,
100 Companies Receiving the Largest Dollar Volume of Prime Military
Contracts (annual publication); the source for the data on domestic
new orders of machine tools are the same as in Table 11.

Note: Postwar recessions included in the above chart are 1957-1958,
1960-1961, 1969-1970 and 1973-1975.

*Military contracts are expenditures that go directly to defense contractors
(who have predominantly been large, U.S. corporations) primarily for the
procurement of military goods.

the military's role in helping to reduce machine tool demand became more apparent. That metalworking consumers had less capital available to invest in new equipment after military contracts declined undoubtedly helped to curtail new orders of machine tools, given the tendency for users to retain their old equipment.

Another important matter must be mentioned in regard to the military's impact on machine tool demand. Following large increases in defense spending that heightened machine tool demand have come times when the military has reduced its holdings of metalworking equipment. Consumers of metalworking equipment most definitely found used military-owned machine tools to be more cost-attractive than new equipment. The problem for machine tool builders was that they had to compete with the military in the market during periods when the demand for their products had already been impaired by reduced defense spending, analogous to what occurred after World War II. Since the military's tools sold for less than new ones, machine tool demand, besides suffering from reduced arms spending and its generalized effects on the business cycle, had been weakened at times by the Department of Defense's selling of its used metalworking equipment. The following passage quoted from a late 1978 Army study of the machine tool industry substantiates what has just been said here:

Government policies in procurement of machine tools have contributed to the cyclical problems of the industry. During times of mobilization the government enters the market for machine tools in a large way. The large influx of orders creates an overload situation on the machine tool industry and also results in a large inventory of machine tools in the hands of the government and their contractors. As the mobilization winds down, the government policy of liquidating surplus equipment throws a large portion of this inventory on the market in direct competition with the firms manufacturing new equipment. Thus, the manufacturers are faced with not only a downturn in defense related business, but the competition from the large volume of used machine tools thrown on the market. Several cycles of this nature have occurred since World War II.[17] (Emphasis added.)

It is possible to get a more specific indication of the relationship between military spending and machine tool demand. Since the aerospace industry, a very large consumer of metalworking equipment, has occupied the paramount position in the military-industrial complex during the postwar years, it is useful to ex-amine machine tool demand in this context. But before doing this it is necessary to show in more detail the importance of the aerospace industry to machine tool demand. Along with estab-lishing the fact that the aerospace industry is one of the major consumers of machine tools (see Table 12), we have also indi-cated in Chapter 3 that aerospace manufacturers are very big users of high-technology metalworking equipment, such as nu-merical control, computerized numerical control, and direct nu-merical control machines. The aerospace industry in the late 1970s maintained over 14% of the more expensive numerical control (NC) tools in use in the country, more than any other single industry. In addition to this, a large number of the far more numerous metalcutting machine tools less than ten years of age in the aerospace industry, as of the late 1970s, were NC tools—23.4% for the aircraft and parts sector and 18% for the guided missiles and space vehicles sector. The other major in-dustrial consumers of machine tools listed in Table 12 each had a much smaller percentage of their metalcutting machine tools less than ten years old equipped with NC technology. For these other machine tool consumers, the percentages are as follows: metalworking machinery, 8.1%; miscellaneous machinery, 8.8%; general industrial machinery, 7%; motor vehicles, 2.6%; and fabricated structural metal products, 5.4%.[18]

The aerospace industry is presently the third largest consumer of technologically advanced machine tools. But despite its de-cline, the aerospace industry still has the largest percentage of metalcutting NC tools under ten years of age among the top six consumers listed in Table 12.[19] In short, this industry for some time has recognized the need to keep equipped with relatively new and modern high-technology machine tools. The fact that this industry is heavily dependent on military contracts has clearly been a major reason for its continued capital investments in advanced machine tools.

The importance of the aerospace industry to machine tool demand is further indicated by looking at the metalworking business of Cincinnati Milacron, the biggest U.S. builder and also the world's leading metalcutting producer. According to a top Milacron official, the aircraft industry accounted for 27% of the company's machine tool orders in 1979. This was nearly two times more than the automotive industry, Milacron's second largest customer.[20]

Having seen in some detail the importance of the aerospace industry to machine tool demand, let us now turn to the examination of the relationship between military spending, aerospace producers, and metalworking demand. Eight very large aerospace producers were selected—Boeing, Grumman, Lockheed, McDonnell Douglas, Rockwell International, Northrop, United Technologies, and General Dynamics—who received sizeable defense subsidies during the 1958–1977 period. The purpose was to ascertain the strength of the relationship between the prime military contract awards that went to these companies and the cyclical domestic demand of the machine tool industry. For the period studied, the correlation coefficient measuring this relationship is .6297.[21]

At this time it is again necessary to refer to the previously cited study completed by the Army on the machine tool industry. The Army's study not only acknowledges that changes in military spending have contributed to the cyclical business of the machine tool industry but also that fluctuations in aerospace expenditures have had the same effect.[22] Somewhat relevant here is the comment made by the editor-in-chief of the *American Machinist*, Anderson Ashburn, who when discussing the business condition of the machine tool industry in early 1971 (that is, just after the 1969–1970 recession) remarked the following: "Anybody who was a heavy supplier to the aerospace industry is in trouble."[23] This statement was probably not made in direct reference to military spending; nonetheless, the fact remains that the total defense contracts that went to the eight large aerospace producers used in the above measurement had been declining for about two years prior to 1971, and this appears to have contributed to the reduction of domestic new orders of machine tools, especially after also considering the indirect effects on other metalworking consumers.

It seems reasonable to assume that new orders for machine tools were likely to increase as long as the defense funds that

went directly to aerospace producers (that is, big military contractors) and then indirectly to other metalworking users were
available to cover the costs of this new equipment. When military
contracts declined, on the other hand, it is likely that aerospace
producers, their subcontractors, and other metalworking users
ordered fewer new machine tools since not as many defense
dollars were in circulation in the economy. Moreover, even the
anticipation of reduced defense dollars from military contracts
can account for declines in new machine tool orders, for such a
psychological effect dampens the expansion initiatives of private-sector manufacturers. If we recall that machine tool users
have been reluctant to replace their old equipment, it seems
logical that reduced military contracts intensified this disincli-
nation for aerospace producers and also for other metalworking
users indirectly affected by these expenditures. The quite strong
relationship between the military contracts that have been
awarded to these large aerospace producers and domestic machine tool demand, therefore, is very realistic when viewed in
the above context.

Despite the recognition of the contribution the military has
made to metalworking demand, the Army's study maintains that
the peacetime impact of defense spending on the machine tool
industry during the 1974–1977 period was an estimated 6%.[24]
Quite correctly this study (which generally is a very good analysis of the machine tool industry) attributes about 1% of this
figure to direct military procurement from the machine tool industry. This part of the 6% figure is not an estimate. It represents
the average for the years 1974–1977 of military contracts for machine tools as a percentage of total new orders of machine tools.
It is the remaining and estimated 5% of the Army's figure which
is highly questionable. This 5% figure is actually the average of
defense purchases as a percentage of the gross national product
(GNP). This figure supposedly represents machine tool demand
generated by defense spending in addition to the equipment the
Department of Defense has procured directly from builders. In
different words, this figure allegedly represents the total indirect
effect of military spending on machine tool demand during the
mid to late 1970s as a result of orders placed by defense contractors and due to defense purchases in general.

In private correspondence with one of the authors of the Army's study I learned that their interest was merely to look for an "order of magnitude statistic." More importantly I learned that their estimate (the 5% figure) included the "far-reaching statistical assumption that defense purchases constitute a random sample of GNP in so far as machine tool usage ratios are concerned." In other words, The Army's study has made the clearly mistaken assumption that machine tool consumption has been roughly equal throughout the entire economy. Additionally, if defense purchases as a percentage of the GNP estimate the impact of military spending on the machine tool industry, then by implication this should be true also for many other, if not all, industries as well.

In regard to consumption, as already indicated, the metal-working, durable goods producing industries have been the biggest users of machine tools. Without any doubt the durable goods industries (such as the automobile, the aerospace, and the fabricated metal products industries) have a much greater need for machine tools than the nondurable goods industries (like the food, the clothing, and the fabrics industries). Concerning the more or less common effects military expenditures have on many sectors of the economy as the Army's study implies, it has definitely not been the case that defense spending has had a generally equivalent impact on different industries. Some industries have occupied strategic positions within the military-industrial complex, making the impact of defense spending on them greater than it has been for others. Regarding the distribution of military contracts, the aerospace, the electronics and telecommunications, the ordnance, and the shipbuilding industries have been the biggest recipients.[25]

Plainly, for many aerospace producers, who have been foremost in and indispensable to the military-industrial complex, defense contracts as a percentage of total sales have been considerably higher than 5%. For example,, this statistic in 1976 for McDonnell Douglas was 69%, while for Grumman it was 65%. Indeed, it is clear that the implication found in the Army's study that defense purchases as a percentage of the GNP are indicative of the military's impact on the private sector as a whole certainly does not hold up well for big aerospace producers. The military's impact on big aerospace producers has been much greater than defense purchases as a percentage of the GNP, which strongly suggests that it could have a somewhat larger effect on the machine tool industry than maintained by the Army's study; to some extent through the aerospace manufacturers themselves.

In order to determine if the impact of military spending on machine tool demand has been greater than suggested in the Army's study, however, one must produce a better statistic than defense purchases as a percentage of the GNP. Prime military contract awards (which, again, represent money going directly to arms contractors primarily for weaponry) as a percentage of the durable goods sector of the GNP is a far more indicative measurement of the estimated annual impact defense expenditures have had on machine tool demand than defense purchases as a percentage of the entire GNP. Using military contracts instead of defense purchases eliminates most service expenditures (such as compensation to Defense Department personnel and military assistance to foreign governments) that are included in the latter outlays. It may be partly true, however, that if we eliminate most service purchases we also reduce some of the impact of military spending on the machine tool industry, since service expenditures have had a stimulating effect on the economy and so probably have created a little metalworking demand. Yet the more conservative usage of prime military contract awards places emphasis primarily on the construction of weapons systems for the Department of Defense.

Using the durable goods industry component of the GNP removes those industries and sectors of the economy where machine tool consumption has not been too great, and so it makes for a more reasonable basis from which to estimate metalworking demand. Thus the use of the durable goods sector of the GNP changes the "far-reaching statistical assumption" found in the Army's study into one that is much more credible.

Table 14 provides much more refined estimates of the average impact of military spending on durable goods producers, including the machine tool industry. Table 14 strongly suggests that the impact of military spending on the machine tool industry during most of the postwar period has been significant. In particular, Table 14 suggests that the impact of military spending

Table 14. Military Contracts as a Percentage of the Durable Goods Industry Sector of the GNP, 1951–1978

Year		Year		Year	
1951	72.6%	1960	25.6%*	1969	23.9%*
1952	56.5	1961	27.9	1970	21.4
1953	31.3*	1962	28.0	1971	19.3
1954	21.9	1963	26.5	1972	19.3
1955	20.4	1964	23.9	1973	16.1*
1956	28.2	1965	20.5	1974	17.1
1957	24.4*	1966	25.7	1975	19.0
1958	31.3	1967	29.4	1976	17.5
1959	27.8	1968	26.6	1977	18.1
				1978	18.8

Sources: Data on military contracts from 1951-1956 from Business Conditions Digest, December 1969, appendix, series 625; the source for military contracts from 1957-1978 is the same as noted in Chart 7. The durable goods components of the GNP from the Economic Report of the President (1984), p. 232.

Table 15. Estimated Annual Portion of Military-Induced Domestic Machine Tool Demand, 1970–1978

(dollars in millions)

Year		Year	
1970	156.9	1975	202.2
1971	144.2	1976	343.2
1972	240.3	1977	490.3
1973	365.1	1978	741.5
1974	373.6		

Note: The figures in this table were approximated by multiplying the estimates in Table 14 for the years 1970-1978 by domestic new orders of machine tools for these same years. (The figures in this table do not include direct military procurement of machine tools.)

on the machine tool industry has been at least three times greater than the 5% estimate found in the Army's study. Note too the *declining* significance of military procurement contracts on the durable goods industry component at the outset of recessions (marked by * in Table 14).

It has certainly been the case for some durable goods producers that military contracts have had a larger impact on their business than suggested by the figures in Table 14, while for others, defense-generated demand has been smaller. Aerospace producers, as already made clear, exemplify this former category, while automobile manufacturers are representative of the latter group. These figures listed in Table 14 more than likely come close to approximating demand engendered by defense contracts for the machine tool industry, especially during peacetime, since although its products have been essential to military production, tool builders have not generally received large orders directly from the Department of Defense. If anything, the percentages in Table 14 are underestimates, given the many machine tools required to sustain and continuously modernize America's immense military apparatus.

A previously cited study prepared for the U.S. Arms Control and Disarmament Agency estimated that for the years 1964–1966 military spending generated approximately 20% of the demand of the machine tool industry.[26] Although noting that military-induced business could not be exactly determined, the authors of this study concluded that the machine tool industry is probably more dependent on defense spending than others within the metalworking machinery industry. It is significant to note here that the approximation of defense dependence given by the authors of this study for the period 1964–1966 is close, for these same years, to the figures listed in Table 14. That is, the average for the years 1964–1966 of the percentages listed in Table 14 is 23.4%, not too different from the estimate cited above.

Though it is probably true that military spending became less important to machine tool demand during the 1970s than in the two preceding decades, nevertheless its impact on the relatively small machine tool industry was certainly not insignificant. Table 15 estimates the annual dollar amount of domestic machine tool business for the years 1970–1978 attributable to defense spending. Considering the annual size of total prime military contract awards (for example, in fiscal year 1978, they amounted to $59,581,864,000), the figures in Table 15, while certainly not exaggerated ones, probably roughly approximate the extent of new machine tool orders generated by these expenditures.

Thus, unlike the Army's study which utilized a rather implausible measurement to arrive at the conclusion that the "peacetime military consumption of machine tools remains a minor factor in the market,"[27] the major points to be emphasized here are very different. In short, the military's share of the machine tool market had been greater than indicated in the Army's study during the 1970s; moreover, it had been markedly greater during the earlier postwar period. Given the many machine tools needed for military production, as already noted, and by virtue of the fact that a war economy has been a permanent feature in the U.S. since the Korean War, these conclusions seem all the more tenable, even though the civilian market had been more important. It now becomes evident that not only did military spending help to precipitate both the good and the bad times of the machine tool industry, as even the Army's study has accurately recognized, but also that the demand created by defense expenditures should not be viewed as an unimportant component of the market. Probably most damaging to machine tool demand had been the fact that reductions in defense expenditures occurred at most inopportune times; cutbacks in military contracts since after the Korean War up to the recession of 1973–1975 preceded each economic downturn.[28] This means that reductions in military contracts, which weakened machine tool demand, combined with the historically disastrous effects of economic downturns to curtail substantially the business activity of tool producing companies. So for example, when the automobile industry experienced declines in new car sales during recessions along with a general weakening of the private sector, and combining all this with the direct and many indirect effects resulting from reduced military expenditures, the business conditions of the machine tool industry had invariably been disastrous. Both economic slowdowns and the state-regulated reductions in military contracts (exacerbated even more during those times when the Department of Defense sold its used machines) which preceded them, in short, adversely impacted upon the business of the machine tool industry.

One final point should be made concerning the contents of the Army's study on the machine tool industry. Although noting the military's contribution to metalworking cycles, what is noticeably absent from the Army's study is a discussion of the long-term effects of defense spending on the machine tool industry. It is extremely important to point out that the very cyclical nature of the machine tool industry, as well as its other problems discussed in Chapter 3, did not just appear all of a sudden. Since the business cycle has been the machine tool industry's biggest problem and because defense expenditures had been closely related to it for some time, for this latter reason alone military spending should be considered injurious. This is so since it means that fluctuating military expenditures contributed to the weakening of the machine tool industry relative to its major foreign competitors, at least up until the 1973–1975 recession. The weakening of the machine tool industry, resulting to some extent because of the adverse effects of the business cycle, which, in turn, has been a contributing factor in the creation of other problems, has been a long-term and cumulative process. The growth of imports and the decline of the machine tool industry's technological lead over its competitors, for instance, have been in the making for some time, even though they have appeared more critical in recent years. The long-term and cumulative impact of military spending on the machine tool industry, in brief, is indeed too important a matter to be overlooked, as the authors of the Army's study have done in their work.

RECENT TRENDS IN MACHINE TOOL DEMAND

From 1976 to 1979 domestic machine tool demand grew steadily. Two of the biggest consumers of machine tools during this period were the automobile and the aerospace industries, though the construction equipment industry contributed somewhat to increasing demand.[29] Automobile producers were consuming large quantities of machine tools primarily because the increased demand for smaller, more fuel-efficient cars necessitated retooling within the industry. The strong demand for machine tools within the aerospace industry resulted from record purchases of civilian planes. Sizeable and growing military contracts to aerospace producers also intensified the consumption of machine tools within the aerospace industry.[30] (In June of 1980 the president of Cincinnati Milacron, while discussing the prospects of his company for the next few years, commented that the first opportunity for future growth comes from the aircraft industry, and that "On top of the boom in commercial planes, the production of military aircraft is expected to increase. This also affects Milacron.")[31] Moreover, it should be noted that annual and steady increases in military contracts in general, especially from fiscal year 1976, were favorable to the boom business of the machine tool industry. In brief, though the private sector was an obvious plus factor concerning the propitious business climate experienced by tool builders, the military's role was not an inconsiderable one during the second half of the 1970s.

Coinciding more or less with this increase in machine tool demand, to some extent engendered by military expenditures, had been the gradual appearance, mainly among the larger builders, of computer-aided design (CAD) and computer-aided manufacturing (CAM). A few years before, the Department of Defense decided it would lead manufacturing industries into CAD/CAM.[32] By the latter part of the 1970s the larger tool builders, and less frequently smaller ones, began using CAD/CAM.[33] The benefits of CAD/CAM for tool builders have been more efficiency and accuracy in designing and producing machine tools. So it would seem that CAD/CAM made at least a minimal contribution in regard to meeting increases in machine tool demand in the second half of the 1970s by helping to better organize metalworking production.

The two recessions in the 1980s severely curtailed domestic machine tool demand. With the heightened military spending that has become obvious in the last few years there has been the need for more machine tools. At the end of the fourth quarter of 1983, when domestic new orders for machine tools were at about the same depressed level they were at in the fourth quarter of 1981, it was acknowledged that military contractors would be ordering many new machine tools.[34] This explains why the aerospace industry has continued to be a major customer of the machine tool industry. The automobile industry has also been a big customer of machine tool builders of late.

Technological trends are expectedly becoming more salient in machine tool use. Numerically controlled tools, consisting of numerical control, computer numerical control, direct numerical control, and manual data input machines, have increased in use from the mid to late 1970s until 1983. There are presently over 103,000 numerically controlled machine tools owned by U.S. industries. In short, the use of numerically controlled machine tools has increased by 95% during recent years. Perhaps the newest machine tool technology, though presently not in widespread use, is flexible manufacturing systems. (See footnote 38, Chapter 3.)

FROM MILITARY-KEYNESIANISM TO SUPPLY-SIDE MILITARISM

While most of the postwar years were characterized by fluctuating military contracts, this policy has been superseded by what clearly is a protracted period of increasing defense spending. Military-Keynesian and demand-side policy have been replaced by supply-side militarism. The latter policy emphasizes that government should play as little a part as possible in the economy. However, the desire for a restricted government applies primarily to social programs. According to the supply-side position, "the need for a buildup in defense spending is widely recognized."[35] By combining rhetoric and politics the supply-side has been able to effectively minimize the glaring contradiction between heightened military spending and the supply-side principle of a retrenched government.

From the end of 1979 until the end of 1982 military contracts increased by more than 100%. At the end of 1983 defense prime contract awards were 60% higher than they were at the end of 1980.[36] Significantly, military contracts did not decline before the two recessions occurring in the early 1980s. With strict military-Keynesianism dormant in the 1980s, the supply-siders, whose theory gained federal recognition during the Carter administration[37] but has come to fruition during the Reagan administration, have been continuously pressing for growing defense expenditures.

As indicated earlier in this chapter (see Table 11) the back-to-back recessions of 1980 and 1981–1982 really harmed the domestic business of the U.S. machine tool industry. In fact, the industry did not really start to recover from these recessions, which began to noticeably reduce domestic new orders of machine tools in the third quarter of 1980, until 1984. Thus the argument advanced that there was actually only one recession, as opposed to the two officially recorded, from 1980 to 1982 gains some credibility when one observes the domestic new orders of the U.S. machine tool industry.

In any case, although the technological benefits of government spending could have been put to much better use in the civilian sector, the continuous increases in military spending during the early 1980s were beneficial to durable goods producers, helping to dampen the impact of recession. In other words, without increases in military spending the machine tool industry would have experienced even worse times, making it even more susceptible to the danger posed by foreign builders.

As military contracts have continued to increase in the 1980s machine tool builders have been quick to point to the stimulus they provide to their business.[38] Not surprisingly in this period marked by increasing military spending, Data Resources, Inc., a leading economic consulting firm, very recently indicated that "by conservative estimate, up to 20 percent of the aggregate domestic consumption of machine tools is related to defense needs even in peacetime."[39] The irony here is a military (demand) stimulus being applied within the context of a supply-side policy which dictates that the least amount of government supposedly yields the biggest benefits.

The machine tool industry has used this period of military growth to pressure government to restrict the persistent threat of imports. A recent petition to the government by the National Machine Tool Builders' Association maintains that "the national security of the United States is being impaired by current levels of imports of machine tools because such imports threaten to debilitate the domestic machine tool industry, which is critical to the United States' defense and deterrence posture.[40] (See

Chapter 5.) Nonetheless, as long as military expenditures continue to expand, the machine tool industry will derive some short-term benefits, since business is clearly stimulated by defense spending.

THE DECLINE OF THE U.S. MACHINE TOOL INDUSTRY AS THE WORLD'S LEADING PRODUCER

The last chapter pointed out that in the early 1970s the West German machine tool industry ascended to the position of the world's leading producer nation. At this time the U.S. had just passed through its fifth postwar recession. Also indicated in the last chapter was that because of the 1969–1970 recession productivity within the machine tool industry decreased significantly. What needs to be made clear here is that military expenditures started declining in fiscal year 1968, and continued until fiscal year 1971. Between fiscal years 1968 and 1970 military contracts decreased by over 19%. During the same time, shipments of U.S. machine tools began to noticeably decrease. From 1968 to 1970 total shipments of machine tools fell by over 16%; while domestic shipments, declining more precipitously, decreased by almost 21%. As military contracts decreased by 5% between fiscal years 1970 and 1971, domestic machine tool shipments declined by 32% from 1970 to 1971.[41] Thus the detrimental effects of the 1969–1970 recession, which further aggravated what was already poor productivity, and declining military contracts, which started to decrease as the U.S. began scaling down from the Vietnam War, together greatly weakened the demand for machine tools.

Because the government of West Germany had devoted relatively little to military spending during the postwar years, the country's machine tool builders did not have to fear reductions in these expenditures, let alone decreased defense spending due to demobilization from a war. Moreover, the West German machine tool industry, which had continued to grow stronger as the postwar years wore on, was experiencing extremely good business conditions until 1972. West German machine tool production, unaffected by a recession until 1972 (and at that time total output declined only minimally) was actually still growing for a short time as American and even Japanese builders experienced a steep slump.

As Chart 8 makes clear, the period 1970–1971 marks the U.S. machine tool industry's formal decline to a secondary status in respect to total output by individual capitalist nations. Thus not only did the U.S. undergo a major military defeat in the Vietnam War along with a decline in global hegemony, but American machine tool builders likewise suffered a major loss due to this war. To say that reduced defense expenditures played only an incidental role in helping to determine the fate of the U.S. machine tool industry during the period of 1970–1971 would be to deny the strong relationship between decreasing military spending and weakened machine tool demand.

Even though military contracts have continued to grow in recent years this has not been a sufficient stimulant to machine tool demand. An International Trade Commission study recently concluded that the Japanese industry's ascension as the leading machine tool producer in the world is "in part, a result of more than 20 years of [Japanese] government intervention in the machine-tool industry."[42] As they have in other high-technology industries in the civilian sector, the Japanese have been able to produce sophisticated and efficient machine tools with government assistance.

MACHINE TOOL DEMAND IN WEST GERMANY AND JAPAN

It is generally known that military spending in West Germany and Japan, unlike in the U.S., has not been exorbitant since World War II.[43] But is is more important to note that because the actual procurement of weapons has understandably been even smaller than total military spending in West Germany and Japan, the overall defense impact on machine tool demand in these countries since the Second World War has been minimal. Put differently, the relatively small military procurement expenditures in West Germany and even smaller in Japan have precluded any substantial postwar relationship between domestic machine tool demand and defense spending in these countries.

Chart 8. U.S., West German, and Japanese Machine Tool Production, 1969–1983

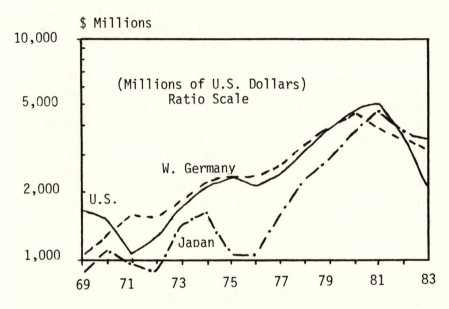

Source: NMTBA, <u>1984-1985 Handbook</u>, p. 164.

In Japan where military expenditures have been almost non-existent, it is clear that nearly all domestic machine tool demand during the entire postwar period has stemmed from the private sector and certainly not from defense spending. The fact that the Japanese machine tool industry's exports have increased rapidly is also indicative of its largely nonmilitary-created demand. For example, exports as a percentage of total machine tool production in Japan increased from 7.2% in 1964 to 16.1% in 1974, and were 39.5% in 1980. In 1983 exports as a percentage of output in Japan stood at nearly 34%.[44] Relatively low arms expenditures in West Germany and even lower weapons procurement expenditures have meant little defense-generated metalworking business. Coupling this fact with the unusually large volume of West German machine tool exports suggests the lack of any really significant demand created by domestic arms spending. From 1960 to 1969 the average of exports as a percentage of total machine tool production in West Germany was 54%; through the 1970s this statistic grew to about 64%. In the 1980s exports as a percentage of production have averaged about 62%.[45] In brief, domestic machine tool demand in both West Germany and Japan has definitely resulted largely from the needs of civilian production; in regard to the foreign business of the machine tool industries in these countries, it is more than likely true that an insignificant amount of their world exports have been used for military purposes. Moreover, it must be pointed out that the relatively lower prices of foreign machine tools, particularly those from Japan, have meant that military and civilian slowdowns in the U.S. have not been as harmful to overseas builders as they were to American producers.

Thus without much demand created by defense spending, West German and Japanese builders have not had to contend with the additional problem of military-assisted cycles in their business activity, unlike the case for their U.S. rivals throughout most of the postwar period. In other words, West German and particularly Japanese machine tool builders have only had to deal with civilian-induced cycles. Not having experienced excessive military spending and its effects on demand has been advantageous to the machine tool industries in West Germany and Japan, since the negative impact of their domestic business cycles have not been intensified by fluctuating defense expenditures.

DEALING WITH THE BUSINESS CYCLE

Increasing exports is doubtlessly the most desirable way to counterpoise the very damaging effects of the business cycle on the machine tool industry. The last chapter, however, made clear the decreasing strength of U.S. tool builders in the world export market. Since exports have not been able to check the negative impact of the business cycle on the machine tool industry some builders have had to rely more so on other less effective counteracting measures. Three major counteracting measures have been the following: (1) diversification; (2) mergers and acquisitions; and (3) investing abroad.

The benefits derived from diversification are clear-cut. Because machine tool demand weakens when the economy slows down, those companies with a diversified product line have somewhat of a built-in cushion protecting them from more serious reductions in their business. Put differently, some machine tool firms have attempted to obviate precipitous recessionary declines in their sales and profits through product diversification. Since sales in other products have not been as likely to decline as enormously as those for machine tools, to some extent diversified companies have defended themselves against what would be exacerbated reductions in their business activity.

For reasons that are rather obvious, large machine tool companies have been more inclined to diversify their business, Cincinnati Milacron, the nation's largest machine tool company, in 1983 had almost 50% of its revenues coming from products other than machine tools.[46] Other big machine tool producers such as Brown and Sharpe and Ex-Cell-O are still further examples of firms with diversified product lines.[47]

Mergers have for some time changed the machine tool industry. Recently, mergers[48] and acquisitions have been affecting machine tool companies. For example, the expected acquisition by Cross & Trecker—itself the result of a merger between the Cross Company and Kearney & Trecker—of Bendix followed shortly after Bendix's 1980 acquisition of Warner & Swasey. In

August of 1982 AMCA International Corporation, an engineering and construction services company, acquired Giddings & Lewis.

Mergers and acquisitions occurring between machine tool companies increase the financial holdings of the companies involved and in this way strengthen their competitive position in the machine tool market. The larger the company and the more sales activity it has, the better it is equipped to weather the harmful effects of the business cycle. Though demand still weakens during economic slowdowns, the significant increase in business during good times and the large backlogs that result during these periods do help to counteract the business cycle to some extent. Just as importantly, these newly formed companies, because of the increase in their finances, have created the potential for diversification which is an added and more effective way to combat the business cycle.

Some machine tool firms have also found investing abroad, either through establishing branch plants or by licensing foreign producers, to be somewhat advantageous. According to the U.S. Department of Commerce, American machine tool builders initially invested abroad to acquire the benefits of lower production costs in foreign countries while also gaining a larger share of the world market.[49] This additional source of profits helped to compensate for reduced domestic demand during economic slowdowns. As foreign production costs have grown and as overseas builders have become stronger and more competitive, the compensating effect of foreign investments has probably declined over the years. Nonetheless, a fairly large number of machine tool companies do maintain facilities abroad; at the same time, some joint ventures between U.S. builders and foreign producers have occurred in recent years.[50]

It is important to reemphasize here that neither product diversification, mergers and acquisitions, or investing abroad can have the same compensating effect as would gaining a larger share of the world export market. And since acquiring a bigger portion of the global export market does not seem to be too likely in the immediate future, downturns in the domestic business cycle, as in the past, will continue to be very problematic for tool builders.

CONCLUSION

This chapter has analyzed the demand component of the very cyclical U.S. machine tool industry during much of the postwar period, with special emphasis placed on the military's contribution to it. Without any doubt civilian production has created the majority of the demand of the machine tool industry. But this is not to say that military expenditures have not generated a fairly significant amount of machine tool demand in the U.S. throughout most of the postwar years, even though some tool builders have had less of their business created by defense spending than others. For indeed it has been argued and demonstrated in this chapter that machine tool demand in the U.S. from the Korean War to the late 1970s had annually depended to varying degrees on military expenditures, while at the same time there had been a strong, long-term and cyclical relationship between them.

Despite continuing efforts mostly by some of the larger U.S. builders to offset the harmful effects of the business cycle, this very critical and extremely debilitating problem has not only persisted, but it has also helped to undermine the machine tool industry in other connected ways; this includes its ability to compete effectively with its major foreign rivals. Significantly, West German and Japanese machine tool builders have ultimately benefited from the fact that their domestic business cycles have not been compounded by internal problems engendered by excessive military spending.

NOTES

1. U.S. Department of Commerce, *U.S. Industrial Outlook 1974*, p. 324.

2. Calculated from NMTBA, *1978–1979 Handbook*, p. 85 and the U.S. Bureau of the Census, *Historical Statistics of the United States, Colonial Times to 1970, Bicentennial Edition*, Washington, D.C., 1975, p. 224.

3. See *Production Engineering*, August 1978, p. 39; "Order Books Filling Up for More Machine Tools," *Iron Age*, March 28, 1977, p. 32.

4. See Standard & Poors, *Industry Surveys, Machinery*, May 27, 1976, p. M 19.

5. Data on machine tool users from "The 13th American Machinist

Inventory of Metalworking Equipment 1983," *American Machinist*, November 1983, pp. 118–19.

6. "Defense Contract Seekers Eye Future Fiscal Plans," *Iron Age*, July 9, 1979, p. 32.

7. Of the three companies that were not major aerospace producers, two firms still had been awarded contracts to produce some aerospace equipment. See *100 Companies Receiving the Largest Dollar Volume of Military Prime Contract Awards, Fiscal Year 1978*, Department of Defense.

8. National Machine Tool Builders' Association (booklet), *Machine Tools/Basic to the Nation*.

9. All data on prime military contract awards for machine tools are from the Department of Defense, OASD (Comptroller), Directorate for Information Operations, *Military Prime Contract Awards by Service Category and Federal Supply Classification*.

10. National Machine Tool Builders' Association (booklet), *Machine Tools/Basic to the Nation*.

11. *Data from NMTBA, 1978–1979 Handbook*, pp. 85–86.

12. Quoted in National Machine Tool Builders' Association (booklet), *Machine Tools/Basic to the Nation*.

13. Abert and McCuistion, *The Defense Dependency of the Metalworking Machinery and Equipment Industry and Disarmament Implications*, p. 168.

14. Ibid.

15. Standard & Poors, *Industry Surveys, Industrial Machinery*, April 22, 1954, pp. M2–5-M2–6.

16. Ibid., p. M2–6.

17. Hintz et al., *Machine Tool Industry Study: Final Report*, p. 26.

18. All data in this paragraph calculated from or found in "The 12th American Machinist Inventory of Metalworking Equipment 1976–1978," *American Machinist*, December 1978, p. 136.

19. See "The 13th American Machinist Inventory of Metalworking Equipment 1983," *American Machinist*, November 1983, p. 118.

20. See *The Wall Street Transcript*, June 23, 1980.

21. From fiscal year 1958 to fiscal year 1966 the figures used in the calculation of this correlation coefficient actually included military contracts awarded to nine aerospace producers. The reason for this is because during this time McDonnell Aircraft Company and Douglas Aircraft Company were still two distinct firms. Due to a merger they became McDonnell Douglas Corporation, and so from fiscal year 1967 to fiscal year 1977 the number of aerospace producers used to compute this correlation coefficient changed to eight.

22. Hintz et al., *Machine Tool Industry Study: Final Report*, p. 14. Of course, the best example of this, as the authors point out, is the period immediately following World War II.

23. Quoted in "A Slowdown that is Hard to Shake Off," *Business Week*, January 30, 1971, p. 19.

24. Hintz et al., *Machine Tool Industry Study: Final Report*, p. 22.

25. Though only a few industries have generally received the bulk of all prime military contract awards, and a small number of big companies within these industries have been the major defense contractors, the concentration of military dollars has been mitigated somewhat through subcontracting and by virtue of the fact that the U.S. economy is interdependent. "Focusing only on prime military contractors is like looking only at the visible part of an iceberg. This represents only the direct impact of the military budget. The indirect impact on subcontractors, on producers of intermediate goods and parts [such as machine tool builders, A.D.], and on suppliers of raw materials ties military spending into the heart of the economy." See Michael Reich, Military Spending and Production for Profit," *The Capitalist System*, Richard C. Edwards et al., eds., (Englewood Cliffs, New Jersey: Prentice-Hall, Inc., 1978), p. 413.

26. Abert and McCuistion, *The Defense Dependency of the Metalworking Machinery and Equipment Industry and Disarmament Implications*, p. 143.

27. Hintz et al., *Machine Tool Industry Study: Final Report*, p. IV. A more recent attempt to estimate military-induced machine tool demand, but only from the DOD and its contractors, can be found in David K. Henry, "Defense Spending: A Growth Market for Industry," in U.S. Department of Commerce, *U.S. Industrial Outlook, 1983*, pp. XXXIX–XLVII; see also Committee, *The U.S. Machine Tool Industry*, pp. 53–54.

28. The only exception to this is when military contracts decreased in fiscal years 1964 and 1965. But even then domestic new orders of machine tools started to decline at the beginning of the minor economic contraction of 1966–67, and by the end of 1967, they had decreased sharply from the previous year. Moreover, the fact that cutbacks in military contracts came prior to the onset of recessions tends to account for delays in the actual distribution of expenditures generated by these contracts. Just as importantly, as indicated in the text, the expectation of reduced defense contracts in the near-term period creates a clear disincentive for business investment. On the other hand, since increases in military contracts have also correlated highly with improved machine tool demand when the economy has been strong, these facts would seem to support the argument that defense spending in the U.S. during the postwar years has been used to help regulate the economy.

29. See Standard & Poors, *Industry Surveys, Machinery*, June 8, 1978, pp. M 25-M 26; and U.S. Department of Commerce/Industry and Trade Administration, *1979 U.S. Industrial Outlook*, pp. 240–41.

30. Cf. "Aerospace Technology Keeps Steady Altitude," *Iron Age*, March 12, 1979, p. 37. The correlation coefficient between military contracts distributed to the eight aerospace producers listed in this chapter and domestic new orders of machine tools covering the period 1958–1978 is .8031 (versus .6297 for the period 1958–1977).

31. See *The Wall Street Transcript*, June 3, 1980.

32. See "Machine Tools in New Era of Change," *Iron Age*, January 8, 1970, p. 74.

33. See "Machine Tool Builders Inch Toward Structural Design," *Iron Age*, November 5, 1979, pp. 83–87.

34. See "A Turnaround May Finally be in the Works," *Business Week*, January 9, 1984, p. 58.

35. Paul Craig Roberts, *The Supply-Side Revolution* (Cambridge, Massachusetts: Harvard University Press, 1984), p. 289.

36. U.S. Department of Commerce, *Business Conditions Digest*, April 1983 and May 1984.

37. See Joint Economic Committee of Congress, *Plugging in the Supply Side* (Washington, D.C.: U.S. Government Printing Office, 1980).

38. See "Machine-Tool Orders Advance But Aren't Brisk," *The Wall Street Journal*, February 27, 1984, p. 6; "Machine-Tool Orders Rose 7% from January," *The Wall Street Journal*, March 26, 1984, p. 2; and "March Orders of Machine Tools Increased 66%," *The Wall Street Journal*, April 30, 1984, p. 4.

39. Quoted in Committee, *The U.S. Machine Tool Industry*, p. 53.

40. Quoted in Committee, *The U.S. Machine Tool Industry*, p. 45.

41. Figure on domestic machine tool shipments calculated from NMTBA, *1978–1979 Handbook*, p. 75.

42. See "U.S. Machine Tools vs. Foreign Competition," *American Machinist*, November 1983, p. 23.

43. Even after total defense spending started to decline as the U.S. was withdrawing from Vietnam, military expenditures in 1971 amounted to 6.9% of the GNP, whereas in West Germany and Japan in this same year, this statistic was 3.3% and .9% respectively. See U.S. Arms Control and Disarmament Agency, *World Military Expenditures and Arms Transfers*, 1967–1976. In 1980 U.S. military spending as a percentage of GNP declined to 5.5%; however, defense expenditures as a percentage of GNP in Japan and West Germany basically remained unchanged. See U.S. Bureau of the Census, *Statistical Abstract of the United States: 1984* (104th edition), Washington, D.C. 1983, p. 883. Increasing defense spending in the U.S. has pushed this figure up at the present time.

44. Calculated from NMTBA, *1984–1985 Handbook*, p. 194.

45. Figures for West Germany calculated from Ibid, p. 186 and NMTBA, *1978–1979 Handbook*, p. 166.

46. See *Moody's Handbook of Common Stocks*, Fall 1984 ed. (New York: Moody's Investor Service, Inc., 1984).

47. Ibid.

48. Some information on merger activity can be found in "Machine Tool Companies Grow Fewer and Bigger," *Iron Age*, January 21, 1980, pp. 23–26.

49. U.S. Department of Commerce, *U.S. Industrial Outlook*, 1968, p. 196.

50. See Committee, *The U.S. Machine Tool Industry*, pp. 4 and 44.

5

The Politics of Survival

Because very few machine tool companies are large enterprises, they understandably lack much individual political clout. Along with serving as a fact- and data-gathering organization for the machine tool industry, the National Machine Tool Builders' Association (NMTBA) has unquestionably acted as the political agency representing a large number of U.S. tool builders. This chapter will examine a few major issues that have politically been very important to the NMTBA. Specifically, this chapter will concentrate largely on the political efforts of the NMTBA to decrease imports and increase both exports and domestic demand. But first it would be helpful to indicate the political relevance of the location of the NMTBA headquarters.

THE POLITICS OF LOCATION

After remaining in Cleveland, Ohio for fifty-five years, the headquarters of the NMTBA moved to Washington, D.C. in 1957. Then in 1971, the NMTBA moved to its present location in McLean, Virginia, which, as the association makes clear, overlooks the nation's capital. Since the latter part of the nineteenth century the state of Ohio has been an important machine tool producing area in the country. But the same cannot be said for Washington, D.C., McLean, Virginia, or the surrounding area, since this region has never been a major center of machine tool production. The movement of the NMTBA headquarters from Cleveland, Ohio to Washington, D.C. and subsequently to just a few miles from the country's capital, therefore, suggests reasons other than those directly connected with the production of machine tools.

Seymour Melman has argued that prompting the relocation of the NMTBA headquarters from Cleveland, Ohio to Washington, D.C. was the fact that the federal government by 1957 owned an estimated 15% of all machine tools in the country. According to Melman, this meant that the federal government possessed about $3 billion worth of machine tools, making it, or more specifically the Department of Defense, the largest single owner at that time.[1] Viewed in this way, the more than fifty years of residence of the NMTBA headquarters in Cleveland, Ohio ended due to political and economic reasons. That is, the implication is that physical proximity, particularly to the Department of Defense, would be both politically and economically practical for the NMTBA since it would increase the likelihood of a smoother relationship between itself and the Pentagon.

Even during more recent years the Department of Defense has maintained a large quantity of machine tools. According to the 1976–1978 metalworking inventory conducted by the *American Machinist*, the federal government possessed 104,107 machine tools and the Department of Defense owned some 96,759 of them; by 1983 the share owned by the Defense Department declined to 63,148.[2] However, the Department of Defense is still probably the largest single owner of this type of equipment, since it is extremely doubtful that any individual company possesses more units than the Pentagon. But it needs to be emphasized here that, in spite of what prompted the move from Cleveland, Ohio, it is very unlikely that the NMTBA headquarters has remained in the Washington, D.C. area from 1957 to the present solely because the Department of Defense owns a large number of machine tools. Possession of machine tools does not indicate the age of this equipment. A 1966 survey of Tooele Army Depot, for example, found that its 152 machine tools were an average age of twenty years old.[3] In 1983 about 86% of the machine tools owned by the Department of Defense were twenty years old or older.[4] This should be expected, given that the preceding chapter pointed out that the Defense Department has generally not been a large, direct annual purchaser of machine tools. Thus, however important the NMTBA believes the possession of a large quantity of machine tools by the Department of Defense to be, there is little doubt that easy access to congressional and other government officials, apart from those in the Pentagon, has been a very important reason for the association's residence in the area of Washington, D.C.

MACHINE TOOL POLITICS: IMPORTS AND EXPORTS

The problem of growing imports coincident with a decreasing share of the world export market has prodded the machine tool industry and the NMTBA for some time now to seek government protection and assistance. Pertaining to exports, the NMTBA has been extremely active in its attempts to reduce and even eliminate most kinds of export restrictions. At the same time, the NMTBA has sought, and been a persistent proponent of, financial assistance by the government in order to promote the exports of the U.S. machine tool industry to all of the countries of the world. The reasoning of the NMTBA concerning exports has been the following: the fewer the export restrictions and the more available export subsidies, the larger the U.S. share of the world market, and consequently, the less damaging domestic business cycle will be to the machine tool industry. Protectionist policies to guard against imports have also been sought by the NMTBA, given the thorough penetration of the U.S. machine tool market by foreign products. In the next three sections more details will be provided on the politics of the NMTBA concerning imports and exports.

Imports

The NMTBA has been staunchly opposed to any form of tariff reductions on imports. Liberalized tariff laws obviously increase the possibility of growing imports, something clearly unwelcomed by U.S. builders. In this respect, the machine tool industry and the NMTBA did not respond favorably to what resulted from the Trade Expansion Act of 1962 and the Kennedy Round negotiations since they both reduced U.S. tariffs (the former by as much as 50%) and set the stage for growing foreign imports of machine tools. In a public statement presented in the late 1960s, the NMTBA regarded the expanded tariff-reducing power of the government of up to 50% "as being, in effect, a subsidy to foreign machine tool builders" since it assisted them in selling their products in the American market.[5]

Before the House Ways and Means Committee in June of 1970 the NMTBA spoke out against any more tariff reductions in addition to those resulting from the Kennedy Round negotiations, which took effect in 1967. Proposed also by the NMTBA at this time, as it had done in the past, was that the government give some thought to imposing a selective import surcharge. But the NMTBA favored another option which it deemed would be more immediately helpful to check the import invasion. Written into the Trade Expansion Act of 1962 was an "escape clause" giving the president the power to reinstitute tariffs to protect those industries harmed by liberalized import tariffs. The NMTBA expressed the view that a more progressive "escape clause" as proposed by the Nixon administration would be the most expedient, effective, and "least controversial" way to guard against imports.[6]

Responding to the alarming growth of imports in more recent years, the NMTBA voiced its opinion in November of 1977 to a House Subcommittee on Trade favoring the strict enforcement of antidumping laws. The NMTBA also supported amendments to antidumping regulations in order to strengthen what it considered to be the "predatory export policies" of foreign machine tool builders. The NMTBA went on to remind this Subcommittee that a large number of small businesses comprise the machine tool industry. For this reason, according to the NMTBA, many machine tool companies have found it difficult to expend their finances on fact-gathering information needed in order "to persuade the Treasury Department to open an investigation" on a violator of antidumping laws. The major and only suggestion proposed by the NMTBA for this financial problem was that the Treasury Department initiate an investigation automatically as a result of a violation of "statutory guidelines"—and indeed these guidelines would clearly have to be heavily biased in order to protect the domestic market from foreign exporters. The essence of the proposed solution by the NMTBA to this matter was that once a Treasury Department investigation was underway, and so all or at least most of the initial costs of gathering the evidence against an alleged violator had been borne by the government, a closer working relationship should be established between the machine tool industry and the Treasury Department. Apparently, the NMTBA, by proposing this suggestion, did not only wish to relieve machine tool builders of the initial investigatory costs, but also to make it easier to prove the charges against foreign producers accused of dumping in the U.S.[7]

Since the products of Japanese machine tool builders have become extremely popular in the U.S., as we have seen in Chapter 3, it is no wonder that accusations of dumping[8] have been leveled at them by the NMTBA.[9] Thus at least one significant outcome stemming from the NMTBA's impassioned charges of dumping by foreign producers in the U.S. was the establishment in March 1978 of the Japan Machinery Exports Association. Japan's Ministry of International Trade and Industry was responsible for beginning this association. The specific function of the Japan Machinery Exports Association is to impose minimum shipping charges on all numerically controlled lathes and machining centers (two of the most expensive machine tools favored by importers of Japanese products) to be exported to the U.S.[10]

At present protectionism is the clarion call of the machine tool industry. The 1981–82 recession brought utter havoc to the U.S. machine tool industry, as imports became more of a threat to domestic producers. By 1983 imports made up about thirty-seven cents of every dollar spent on machine tools consumed in the U.S.; this was up significantly from 1981 and 1982 when imports accounted approximately for between twenty-six and twenty-seven cents out of every dollar. As imports, particularly from Japan, have become more damaging, the American machine tool industry has suffered from what it believes to be the unrestrained and overly aggressive trade practices of its foreign competition. On May 3, 1982 Houdaille Industries, a leading U.S. machine tool company, independently petitioned the government to reduce Japanese imports. Invoking Section 103 of the Revenue Act of 1971, Houdaille asked the Reagan administration to deny investment tax credits to U.S. firms that purchased Japanese NC punching equipment and machining centers. According to Houdaille, Japanese builders have profited from an illegal cartel. The Reagan administration rejected Houdaille's protectionist position in April of 1983.[11]

At the time the Houdaille petition was still pending, the NMTBA mounted a campaign to restrict imports. In March 1983 the NMTBA filed a petition utilizing Section 232 of the Trade Expansion Act of 1962—which gives to the president protectionist powers against foreign competitors endangering the national defense—claiming the machine tool imports are a threat to the country's defense. Many in the Commerce Department apparently felt the petition should be rejected; however, Commerce Secretary Baldrige repudiated the suggestions of his staff and recommended to the White House that almost 90% of all sophisticated machine tool imports should be restricted to the U.S. Opposed by the Council of Economic Advisors, the Office of Management and Budget, the State Department, and the Office of the U.S. Trade Representative, but in agreement with the NMTBA, Baldrige argued that the machine tool industry, which is being bludgeoned by foreign (Japanese) builders, is essential to the national defense.[12] But the chances that the Reagan administration will take a protectionist stance against foreign machine tool imports does not appear to be too good. Nonetheless, the Reagan administration probably pleased the NMTBA when it announced its plan to send Trade Representative William Brock to Tokyo for the purpose of attempting to reduce Japanese subsidies to export industries.[13]

Although machine tool protectionism has been evident, the NMTBA has taken another position. According to the NMTBA, "Over the years, the American machine tool industry has steadfastly remained an outspoken advocate of free trade. . . . We have supported the principle of free, open and fair competition among all of the world's machine tool builders."[14] It seems that a much more practical and accurate argument is that, especially since the import invasion (see Chapter 3), the NMTBA has been less interested in free trade than in making a plausible political case for the partial restoration of the domestic market to U.S. builders, a market that was once their near-exclusive preserve. In its efforts to accomplish this nearly impossible goal, the

NMTBA has deviated at times from the notion of free and open trade by adopting a protectionist line of action.

Exports

Export issues have also been politically important to the NMTBA, as noted above. In the past, the NMTBA had requested that government work to eliminate nontariff trade barriers abroad in order to facilitate U.S. machine tool exports.[15] But more important to the NMTBA in recent years in regard to exports have been matters directly related to the policies of the U.S. government. In this respect, the NMTBA has protested that U.S. restrictions on exports have unduly harmed American machine tool builders.

One major obstacle to U.S. machine tool exports, according to the NMTBA, has been COCOM (Coordinating Committee for Exports to Communist Countries). COCOM is a fifteen-member international organization made up of Western European nations, the U.S., Canada and Japan. Originating in 1949 and based in Paris,[16] this informal organization meets about every three years to examine the lists compiled by member countries concerning what military, nuclear, and other types of strategic equipment should be denied to the communist nations. Though the equipment to be restricted eventually results from an agreement by all members, no legal regulations prohibit individual COCOM participants from exporting to the communist countries. That is, ultimately each COCOM member makes its own decisions about what should be exported to the communist countries. So, as one NMTBA statement before a Senate Subcommittee on International Finance put it, this has meant "that there has not been uniform interpretation of the existing COCOM regulations by all of the participating nations. As a result, it has been the American machine tool industry that has been hit the hardest by COCOM controls."[17] In other words, according to the NMTBA, differential application of COCOM regulations has been very advantageous to the U.S. machine tool industry's foreign competitors since other governments interpret these controls more liberally than the American government. The impact of restrictive COCOM regulations on U.S. machine tool builders has been that at times they have experienced long delays in obtaining the export licenses needed for shipments to communist nations, or they have just been denied permission to transport some equipment to these countries. These last two reasons, from the perspective of the NMTBA, have made the communist machine tool market more accessible to the overseas competitors of American builders (that is, supposedly due to the less restrictive COCOM regulations abroad).[18]

Two additional statements made by the NMTBA concerning COCOM are: (1) neither Sweden nor Switzerland are members of COCOM and both countries produce advanced machine tool equipment which has been transported to communist countries; and (2) denying the communist countries at least some of the machine tool technology possessed by COCOM members has hastened the development of advanced metalworking equipment in these nations. Given the NMTBA's animus toward CO-COM, it is not at all surprising that it has recommended that this organization should be entirely restructured to make it more effective, or abolished altogether.[19] Stringent export controls resulting from the Export Administration Act of 1969 have in the past also contributed, along with COCOM regulations, to reduced shipments to communist countries, according to the NMTBA. In order to strengthen its case, the NMTBA has pointed out that reduced exports have meant fewer jobs for Americans in the U.S. and smaller expenditures for research and development.

Regarding all forms of export controls, basically the NMTBA, voicing the general attitude of machine tool builders, has contended that only if equipment can be proven to be significantly and unequivocally detrimental to the national defense or foreign policy interests of the U.S., while at the same time not available from other noncommunist metalworking producers, should it be considered contraband material. This argument apparently originated owing to the fact that the NMTBA has charged that the principal organization responsible for reducing machine tool exports has been the Department of Defense. The Department of Commerce, which is accountable for the administration of export regulations, has been much less restrictive than the De-

partment of Defense, which has maintained exceptionally restrictive practices concerning machine tool exports to the socialist
countries, as has, to a lesser degree, the Department of Energy.
According to an NMTBA statement before the House Subcommittee on International Economic Policy and Trade, some individuals in the Department of Defense refuse to grant an export
license for any machine tool to be exported to the socialist countries.[20] And when export licenses have been granted, the Department of Defense has been primarily responsible for protracted
delays, which at times, last as long as two years.[21] Asserted a
top official from one of the bigger machine tool producers, Giddings and Lewis, Inc.: "I guess it would be fair to say the Department of Defense in particular has held back business
negotiations when our allies are in there with both feet selling
competitive equipment and we're not permitted to participate.
Licenses have been either refused or delayed so long by individual members of the [Defense] department that we couldn't
be competitive."[22]

An examination of U.S. machine tool exports to the communist
nations, however, shows that American exports to these countries were not extremely hampered, at least not until 1976 when
the Jackson-Vanik Amendment started to have an impact on
American producers. (A detailed discussion of U.S. machine tool
exports to the communist countries after 1975 and the Jackson-
Vanik Amendment will be provided below.) More or less con-
current with the decline in the U.S. machine tool industry's share
of the world export market was an increased interest by the
NMTBA in the socialist market. Midway through the 1960s the
NMTBA's International Trade Committee suggested that the association assist American builders in gaining a larger portion of
the socialist machine tool market. This resulted in an all-out
effort by the NMTBA—including trade missions to socialist
countries along with other promotional techniques—to attempt
to increase U.S. machine tool sales to the communists.[23]

U.S. machine tool exports to the communist countries in the
Eastern Bloc, who steadily increased their consumption of metalworking equipment, grew from $100,000 in 1965 to $18.1 million
in 1969. Even with the institution of the Export Administration
Act of 1969, U.S. machine tool exports to the Eastern Bloc coun-

Table 16. Share of the Eastern Bloc's Non-Communist Machine
Tool Imports Held by Six Major Capitalist Countries,
1962–1980

Year		U.S.	France	West Germany
1962		1.1%	8.4%	34.2%
1965		.2	10.2	26.3
1970		3.1	9.4	36.5
1975		11.3	10.2	39.5
1980		2.8	13.2	44.7
1965-1970	(average)	3.0	11.5	33.1
1971-1975	(average)	7.9	7.9	40.3
1976-1980	(average)	4.6	9.0	43.7

Year		Italy	Japan	Switzerland
1962		23.8%	2.1%	12.0%
1965		14.0	6.6	23.2
1970		15.6	5.0	14.2
1975		8.6	4.3	14.0
1980		12.1	6.8	12.0
1965-1970	(average)	13.7	4.7	16.7
1971-1975	(average)	8.6	8.1	12.9
1976-1980	(average)(b)	10.3	9.5	12.3

Source: NMTBA, 1984-1985 Handbook, p. 231.

(a) Eastern Bloc Countries are Bulgaria, Czechoslavakia, East Germany,
    Hungary, Poland, Rumania and the U.S.S.R.

(b) For 1977 and 1979, Bulgarian imports from the U.S. are excluded;
    for 1978, Czechoslavakian imports from Japan are omitted.

tries had grown to $102.1 million by 1975,[24] with a very large part of the total going to the U.S.S.R. Just how much more rigorously U.S. officials interpreted the COCOM regulations than did the organization's other members, not to even mention the impact of the Export Administration Act of 1969, is difficult to determine precisely from 1965 to 1975. While a rigorous interpretation of export regulations by American officials, especially by those in the Department of Defense, given their preoccupation with world military hegemony, has more than likely been true to some degree, it is nonetheless unambiguously clear that the share of the Eastern Bloc market held by U.S. machine tool builders significantly increased from 1965 to 1975, as can be seen from Table 16. The date in Table 16 also makes evident that while West German builders have for some time dominated the Eastern Block market, the average share of this market individually retained by French, Italian, and Swiss producers actually declined during the years 1971–1975 compared to the period 1965–1970. It is interesting to note here that Italy and France are both members of COCOM.

Given the improvement in American machine tool business with the Eastern Bloc nations from 1965 to 1975, while two other COCOM members during this same period lost some of the socialist market, it seems reasonable to infer that apart from some interference by the Department of Defense, the existence of COCOM and the Export Administration Act of 1969 did not seriously inhibit U.S. metalworking expansion in the communist countries during these years. Owing to the fact that the NMTBA showed little interest in the socialist market prior to the mid–1960s, a very large and sudden increase in U.S. machine tool exports to the Eastern Bloc countries would seem to have been very unlikely; foreign machine tool builders, especially those in West Germany, had already established themselves in the Eastern Bloc market at a time when U.S. producers were just beginning to recognize the consumptive potential of the socialist countries. We must conclude, therefore, that the NMTBA designed its statements dealing with the very rigorous interpretation of COCOM controls by U.S. officials and the strictness of the Export Administration Act of 1969 to liberalize as much as possible, if not totally eliminate, these regulations in order to increase the American share of the communist machine tool market at the expense of the foreign competition. Unfortunately, as we shall see below, the NMTBA has also had to contend with the more recent export restriction of the denial of Export-Import Bank financing to many communist countries. But first, a few comments should be made on the Export-Import Bank and how it has been viewed by the NMTBA.

The Export-Import Bank (Eximbank) is a government organization, established in 1934, that works primarily to ensure U.S. export business. The NMTBA has consistently supported Eximbank. Although the NMTBA has claimed that insufficient Eximbank loans have hindered the competitive opportunities of U.S. tool builders in the world market (that is, because of the better financing supposedly made available for the products of many foreign producers by their governments),[25] it has also maintained nearly the exact opposite. In a statement presented in April of 1974 before a House Subcommittee on International Trade, the NMTBA made the point that "Eximbank has developed financing programs that put us on more equal footing with our foreign competitors."[26] In spite of this contradiction, it is generally true that the less restrictive Eximbank is in regard to subsidizing U.S. exports, the more favorable will be the response of the NMTBA. For example, the NMTBA was pleased with changes leading to the increased accessibility of Eximbank credit, for at one time loans had apparently been denied because of the supposed availability of private funds. The NMTBA also supported Eximbank's stepped-up efforts in the late 1970s to make more loans available for small foreign orders.[27]

The same NMTBA statement of April of 1974 referred to in the preceding paragraph also made clear the objections of the association to proposals then being considered in both the Senate and the House "that would condition the availability of Eximbank financing for sales to a particular foreign country on that country's emigration policies."[28] But despite the objections of the NMTBA, the Jackson-Vanik Amendment came to pass. After its enactment, the NMTBA pointedly and repeatedly appealed to the government to repeal or alter this prohibition.[29]

The Jackson-Vanik Amendment to the Trade Act of 1974 linked America's views concerning what it considered to be the harsh emigration policies of some communist countries to the refusal to grant Eximbank financing to these nations. As a result of this amendment, in the late 1970s only a very small number of communist countries received Eximbank credits on U.S. machine tool exports. The Carter Administration's observance of human rights violations in the communist world compounded the adverse effects of the Jackson-Vanik Amendment on U.S. exports. More damaging at this time was that as American builders' share of machine tool exports to the traditional, noncommunist market was declining, metalworking consumption in the socialist countries, especially in the Soviet Union,[30] was quickly expanding; in 1977 the socialist countries utilized more than 45% of the machine tools consumed outside of the U.S.[31] All in all, from 1975 to 1976 U.S. machine tool exports to the Eastern Bloc countries fell by nearly $40 million, and by the end of 1977 they had declined by another $17.2 million.[32] So no doubt to some indeterminable degree, due to the Jackson-Vanik prohibition, U.S. machine tool exports to this growing socialist market started to decline by 1976.

Resonating to some extent its arguments concerning other export restrictions, the NMTBA underscored the points that strong machine tool exports are good for the U.S. machine tool industry, and at the same time they contribute to a healthy American economy, including more jobs and an improved trade balance. In other words, the only real losers from the Jackson-Vanik Amendment, according to the NMTBA, have been Americans and, of course, the U.S. machine tool industry. It has not been the communist countries that have suffered from the Jackson-Vanik prohibition, maintained the NMTBA, since they have received the equipment they have wanted from foreign machine tool builders. Although these arguments are certainly true, a few more things need to be pointed out.

The dollar value of West German machine tool exports in 1976 increased noticeably to the Eastern Bloc countries, the same year that U.S. exports to this market began to decline. But it is just as noteworthy to point out that the dollar value of French machine tool exports to the Eastern Bloc nations also declined in 1976 from the preceding year, while Italian exports barely increased at all. Put differently, the respective percent shares of the Eastern Bloc market held by French and Italian builders declined in 1976 from the previous year. The fact is that the West German machine tool industry has consistently maintained the largest share of the Eastern Bloc market, as indicated earlier. (See Table 16). Moreover, it is important to note here that two years before the enactment of the Jackson-Vanik Amendment the dollar value of West German machine tool exports had been greatly increasing to the Eastern Bloc nations. It should also be understood that three conditions have been very beneficial over the years to West German machine tool builders and have assisted them in acquiring the largest share of the Eastern Bloc market, apart from the probability of less restrictive export controls: (1) their proximity to these nations; (2) their generally low prices; and (3) their high-quality products that seemingly have satisfied the metalworking needs of the communists.

Thus the major point is that it is not easy to determine how much of the socialist market U.S. producers lost due to the Jackson-Vanik Amendment and how much may have been taken from them by the extremely exported-oriented West German machine tool industry, as it apparently did to French and Italian builders who certainly did not have to contend with this prohibition. Though the Jackson-Vanik Amendment, much more than the COCOM controls and the Export Administration Act (the last, as will be pointed out below, is now more satisfactory to tool builders), has reduced U.S. machine tool exports to the communist countries, it is much too facile to accept the argument of the NMTBA that this prohibition has been so utterly decisive in accounting for the decline in American metalworking sales to the socialist nations. In any event, the very most the U.S. machine tool industry could have expected from the repeal of the Jackson-Vanik Amendment would have been the chance to recapture the 11% noncommunist share of the Eastern Bloc market that it held in 1975.[33]

Unfortunately, the U.S. machine tool industry has been unable to regain its foothold in the Eastern Bloc market. During the 1980s this market will probably all but disappear for U.S. builders. As of 1980, the percentage of the Eastern Bloc's noncommunist imports coming from the U.S. amounted to 2.8%. (See Table 16.)

Moreover, the government's position against extending Eximbank credits to many communist countries that have been denied them because of the Jackson-Vanik Amendment appears steadfast. At the present time a number of socialist countries are not receiving Eximbank financing because of the Jackson-Vanik Amendment. Countries such as the Soviet Union, East Germany, and Czechoslovakia currently receive no Eximbank financing.

Back in the spring of 1978, an advocate of increasing U.S. exports, Senator Adlai Stevenson, urged the NMTBA not to continually attack and criticize the Jackson-Vanik Amendment, but rather to come up with a better alternative to it, in spite of the fact that this prohibition had clearly failed to achieve its stated purpose of bringing about liberalized emigration policies and improved human rights to the communist nations. Expressing his support for what most likely has become the ulterior purpose for maintaining the Jackson-Vanik Amendment probably better than anyone even in the Department of Defense could have, Senator Stevenson reminded the NMTBA of the words of Lenin: "When it comes time to hang the capitalists, they will sell us the rope." Then Senator Stevenson himself remarked that "It didn't occur to him [Lenin] we might even subsidize the sale of the rope."[34] In short, though the Jackson-Vanik Amendment has not brought human rights reform to much of the socialist world from the perspective of the U.S. government, it has served to make synonymous "communism" and the loss of "individual freedom." Such a synonymity helps to justify the existence of this prohibition and, to some extent, a massive military apparatus.

During the summer of 1983, the NMTBA again argued that COCOM has been doing much more damage to the U.S. machine tool industry than it has to the industries of other COCOM members. The NMTBA noted that, excluding the U.S., the communist countries presently account for about 50% of the machine tools consumed in the world. Part of the reason for the failure of the U.S. machine tool industry to penetrate the Eastern Bloc market, according to the NMTBA, is that items found on the U.S. Commodity Control List, and which require export licenses, are not always found on the COCOM list. This means that the U.S. machine tool industry is being hurt by unilateral export controls, primarily as a result of a zealous Defense Department which at the very least delays licensing approvals to the communist countries. The NMTBA favors a retrenchment of the U.S. Commodity Control List. Another part of the problem of the small amount of U.S. machine tools in the Eastern Block market, contends the NMTBA, is that the other COCOM members continue to violate the multilateral export controls of the organization—controls which have been designed so that there will be uniform adherence of export restrictions to the socialist nations. The most effective way to deal with this problem, says the NMTBA, is through the imposition of import restrictions. Specifically the NMTBA supported a proposal to limit imports to the U.S. from countries alleged to be in violation of the multilateral export restrictions found on the COCOM list.[35]

It is important to point out that even if COCOM restrictions are not uniformly followed by all members, the export-oriented West German machine tool industry, in particular, has had a firm grasp on the Eastern Bloc market for some time. In 1980 the West German machine tool industry held almost 45% of the Eastern Block market—over three times more than French producers, the next biggest noncommunist exporter to this market. Taking this market away from West German builders, and to a much lesser extent from French, Italian, and Swiss producers would be a monumental accomplishment for the U.S. machine tool industry in the 1980s.

In short, three major reasons account for the weakness of the American machine tool industry in the Eastern Bloc market. First, the U.S. obsession with military-related matters has placed a salient impediment on this industry through the over cautious export policy of the Defense Department. Second, the Jackson-Vanik Amendment nearly coincided with the onset of the decline in importance of the Eastern Bloc to U.S. builders. Third, and most important, the continued erosion of the U.S. machine tool industry over a number of years, as a result of a defense-industrial policy and fluctuating military spending, severely damaged its overall proficiency. Clearly, export restrictions to the communist countries—supposedly so very detrimental to U.S. producers—do not explain why the American machine tool industry accounted for only 5.3% of West Germany's imports from fourteen nations in 1980, while Swiss producers held 30% of this market and the Japanese had almost 16%. An argument suggesting that unfair export restrictions faced by American builders prevents economies of scale from fully developing is implausible, since a more aggressive export posture toward U.S. allies would have been the appropriate compensating measure. But a review of U.S. machine tool exports, during the 1974–1980 period, to countries such as Japan, France, and Great Britain does not show evidence of this measure being utilized by American builders. In all three of these countries the U.S. export share remained at about the same level in 1980 as it was in 1974.[36]

EXPORT POLITICS AND THE INFLUENCE OF THE NMTBA

Apart from the continuance of the Jackson-Vanik prohibition and COCOM, the NMTBA has been successful over the years in helping to bring about improvements in political matters directly affecting machine tool exports. The political influence of the NMTBA was certainly evident in the establishment of the Technical Advisory Committee for Numerically Controlled Machine Tools. Authorized in January of 1973 due to pressure from the NMTBA, this committee was started to recommend to the Office of Export Administration the kinds of restrictions that should be maintained on numerical control machine tools. The general satisfaction of the NMTBA with this committee was suggested in 1974 when it stated that "Unilateral controls on NC (numerical control) equipment have been virtually eliminated."[37] Continually protesting to the government about the injustices of the Export Administration Act of 1969, moreover, paid off for the NMTBA.

By the end of September 1979 the Export Administration Act of 1979 had been passed by both the Senate and the House. The Export Administration Act of 1979 contained changes clearly favorable to U.S. machine tool exports. Importantly, after 1979 time limits for licensing applications were instituted to expedite exports.[38] The Export Administration Act of 1979 expired at the end of fiscal year 1983 (September 30, 1983). Because the NMTBA has always worked to promote export policies favorable to the industry, the organization strove to make what it considered to be further improvements in the Export Administration Act Amendments of 1983. The NMTBA has noted that this legislation has a direct effect on the American machine tool industry.[39]

CAPITAL RECOVERY AND THE NMTBA

In order to encourage exports and to make American machine tool products more competitive in the world market, the NMTBA has at different times in the past proposed the extensive use by government of indirect taxes (such as value-added taxes) which would provide U.S. builders with rebates for exporting their equipment.[40] The NMTBA has also strongly supported the Domestic International Sales Corporation, which was instituted in 1971 to provide tax concessions to business with the intended goal of stimulating U.S. exports.[41] But apparently most important to the NMTBA in more recent years has been its persistent support for a liberal capital recovery plan for business. If such a plan was made available by the government it would increase, according to the NMTBA, the likelihood that capital investments would be made by individual businesses for production equipment. An effective capital recovery policy from the perspective of the NMTBA, therefore, provides an additional impetus to machine tool demand.

Let us begin by looking briefly at the capital recovery program in the U.S. beginning in the early 1960s. In the latter part of 1961, though not effective until the beginning of 1962, the U.S. government instituted a 7% investment tax credit. The government repealed the 7% investment tax credit in 1966, only to reinstitute it in March of 1967. Once again, in 1969, the 7% investment tax credit was eliminated. By 1971 not only had this tax been reinstated, but the government also enacted a new, more advanced capital recovery program. This program was the 20% Asset Depreciation Range System.

The NMTBA has been quick to point out that up until 1971 the U.S. had the worse capital recovery system of all of the advanced capitalist nations. The reinstatement of the 7% investment tax credit and the beginning of the Asset Depreciation Range System in 1971 greatly improved the U.S. capital recovery program, placing it in about the middle relative to those of other advanced capitalist societies.[42] By 1975, the government had increased the investment tax credit to 10%. This led one consumer of machine tools to remark that "We need a continuance of a minimum 10% investment tax credit if the machine tool industry is to stay competitive with Japan and West Germany."[43] But despite a sustained 10% investment tax credit and the Asset Depreciation Range System, both of which after seven years permitted businesses to recover 103% on the original cost of their production equipment, U.S. machine tool builders still were finding it extremely arduous to compete with West German and Japanese producers. Just as interesting was that in West Germany after seven taxable years, the capital recovery system there in the 1970s formally returned much less to investors than did the one in the U.S., while in Japan the formal return after seven years was only slightly below that received by American businesses.[44] In other words, beginning in 1971 the increased competitiveness of Japanese and West German machine tool builders, the major rivals of U.S. producers, was not due to better capital recovery systems in these countries.

On at least two occasions in the early 1970s the NMTBA linked the twice-repealed 7% investment tax credit to domestic machine tool demand.[45] The NMTBA argued that the presence of an investment tax credit improved domestic machine tool demand, while its absence negatively affected the business of tool builders. It is true that an investment tax credit which in effect reduces the tax liabilities of businesses is somewhat of a stimulant at times to machine tool demand. But it should be made clear that when the economy is strong and prospering, businesses will generally increase their investments in machine tools, notwithstanding an investment tax system, since greater production means larger sales and growing profits. To the degree that this statement is true, an investment tax credit simply rewards businesses for what they would do anyway under propitious economic conditions.[46] Conversely, when the economy is weak businesses will reduce their investments in machine tools whether a capital recovery system is fully intact or not. Thus the point is that the presence or absence of an investment tax credit has been less of a factor in the decisions made by machine tool users to purchase or not to purchase new equipment than the state of the economy; moreover, because of constantly rising machine tool prices, even when the economy has been strong metal-working users have been averse to purchasing too much new equipment.

Looking directly at quarterly domestic new orders of machine tools gives support to the above argument. For example, although the 7% investment tax credit had been cancelled in the fourth quarter of 1966, domestic machine tool demand had already begun declining in the second quarter of 1966. And despite the reinstitution of the 7% investment tax credit in early 1967, domestic machine tool demand did not markedly improve (and at times it even declined) until the last quarter of 1968—a period of about eighteen months. This delay strongly indicates that decisions to purchase new machine tools during the 1967–1968 period did not depend on the availability of an investment tax credit system, since if they were a quicker upturn in domestic machine tool business should have occurred before the end of 1968. Though the suspension of the 7% investment tax credit in 1969 corresponded more closely with declining machine tool demand at that time, its reinstitution, effective in April of 1971, had virtually little impact on improving the business of builders by the end of that year; at the end of 1971 domestic new orders of machine tools increased by less than $14 million from 1970, the worse year of business in eight years.

Further invalidating the argument concerning the relationship between the investment tax credit and machine tool demand is what occurred during the recession of 1973–1975. Contrary to what one would expect from this argument, during the 1973–1975 recession when machine tool demand drastically declined, an investment tax credit, in addition to the Asset Depreciation Range System, remained in operation throughout the entire downturn. Though a much improved capital recovery system persisted, domestic machine tool demand in constant dollars in 1975 was the lowest it had been since 1968.[47] Thus despite the presence of a generous capital recovery system, when the economy weakened businesses withheld much of their investments in new machine tools, especially since the prices of tools continued to markedly increase during the 1973–1975 recession.[48]

On August 13, 1981 the Economic Recovery Tax Act (ERTA) became law, owing to the supply-side initiatives of the Reagan administration. In addition to personal tax cuts, this act greatly reduced business taxes. The ERTA included the Accelerated Cost Recovery System, a capital recovery program which, for the third time since tax depreciation originated in 1954, significantly reduced the depreciation period for productive equipment.

About a year later the Tax Equity and Fiscal Responsibility Act (TEFRA) was passed to curtail the enormity of projected budget deficits. The TEFRA rescinded some of the tax breaks passed under ERTA that were advantageous to investors in equipment; nonetheless, business tax breaks have remained very much intact as a result of Reagan administration initiatives. According to the Urban Institute, "corporate tax liabilities were reduced $10 billion in FY 1983 and are projected to fall by $17 billion in FY 1986 or by 16 percent relative to what they would have been prior to pre-ERTA law."[49]

Indeed, the capital recovery program in 1983 was substantially more generous than the one that previously existed in the U.S. Businesses are capable of recovering almost 80% of the purchase cost of machinery and equipment in the third taxable year—a 12.6% increase from a few years earlier. In the seventh taxable year, as of 1983, machinery and equipment investors can recoup 121.7% of the purchase price, a figure markedly higher than in Japan (80.1%) and in West Germany (91.7%).[50] In short, the formal U.S. capital recovery program is noticeably better than those existing in either West Germany or Japan.

Yet this greatly improved capital recovery program has done little for the machine tool industry. The supply-siders claimed that tax incentives would soon lead to a rejuvenated business environment. With recession gripping the economy for sixteen months, the business climate was hardly auspicious for machine tool builders. In the third quarter of 1982, about a year after the passage of the 1981 business tax breaks, domestic new orders for machine tools reached their lowest point, on a quarterly basis, in almost eleven years. In the last quarter of 1984, in addition to the constant import problem, the machine tool industry was still struggling to make a comeback from the recession. An improved capital recovery program had still not produced the kind of growth the machine tool industry was experiencing in 1979 and the first half of 1980—before the institution of the business tax breaks of 1981. Expressing his feelings about business in late 1984, an executive from Houdaille Industries noted that, while orders have risen from their lows reached during the recession, he "certainly wouldn't describe it as a boom for capital equipment, and if it is, it's mostly for offshore producers."[51] The supply-side capital recovery program has just not sufficiently penetrated all sectors of the economy. Vigorous economic expansion has not been a reality for all American industries.

The NMTBA has also suggested at different times that at least three related benefits would result domestically from a sound capital recovery system in the U.S.: (1) more jobs within the machine tool industry; (2) increased productivity throughout the country; and (3) the replacement of obsolete machine tools.[52] Regarding the first claim by the NMTBA, in October of 1971, a spokesman for the NMTBA and the American Machine Tool Distributors' Association remarked before the Senate Subcommittee on Finance that "On the point of increasing jobs and reemploying people, if the machine tool industry moves once again into its upward cycle with a benevolent tax law, you will find that there will be 118,000 people or more employed once again."[53] The machine tool industry's business cycle did significantly improve beginning in 1972, and it continued to be healthy until 1974. And though the capital recovery system at this time was at least somewhat benevolent, the largest number of workers employed by the machine tool industry during this period was only 94,000—over 20,000 less than the projected target. Even with a more liberalized capital recovery system beginning in 1975 and the resurgence of sales after the 1973–1975 recession, employment in the machine tool industry by 1977 had declined to 84,100. By 1983, despite further improvements in the capital recovery program and economic growth, total employment in the machine tool industry was about 63,000, the lowest number ever reached.

A greatly improved capital recovery system has also not really contributed to the removal of obsolete machine tools from the establishments of metalworking users. Too many aged and a relatively smaller number of young tools are in U.S. factories, as noted in Chapter 3. Nor have improved capital recovery policies proven to be the panacea for the country's productivity problem.

Thus it is clear that a strong capital recovery program (tax breaks) does not produce the claimed results. The fact of the matter is that what is most important to machine tool investors is not capital recovery policies but the condition of the "managed economy" along with the purchasing cost of the equipment, which partly explains the continuation and intensification of the import problem. In the U.S. during the postwar years the management of the economy has been one of the major tasks of the state. Since the 1960s a capital recovery system has been an adjunctive implement used by the state at times to help regulate the economy—an economy that has also been influenced by a military-Keynesian policy. In regard to machine tool demand, we have shown in detail in Chapter 4 that, for a number of years, there has been a very close relationship between fluctuating military contracts and domestic machine tool demand. Yet, from the perspective of the NMTBA, a constantly improving capital recovery system is beneficial to the machine tool industry, and so the association has repeatedly presented its position to the government stressing the need for such a program. For example, at one time the NMTBA advocated a permanent 12% investment tax credit. The NMTBA also supported an increase in the Asset Depreciation Range System, or, alternatively, that depreciable time on capital investments be decreased, especially in those industries where technological change makes equipment obsolete in a relatively short period of time.[54] The passage of the Accelerated Cost Recovery System in 1981 coincided with NMTBA interests, since it reduced the depreciation time for equipment.

THE NMTBA AND THE POLITICS OF FRUSTRATION

Deeply disturbing the NMTBA in the late 1970s was the rejection of a bid made by the Carlton Machine Tool Company of Cincinnati, Ohio to Chrysler for machine tools required for the construction of turrets for XM–1 tanks. Chrysler awarded $2.7

million in late December of 1977 to Mitsubishi Corporation, a Japanese branch plant located in the U.S., and to its American sales agent, Android Corporation. The Defense Department selected Chrysler to be the prime contractor of the $5-billion–plus XM–1 tank project.* Supposedly over 3,000 tanks will be produced for the Department of Defense during the 1980s and 1990s. The Department of Defense supported Chrysler's decision to select foreign producers to construct the needed tools for the turret of the XM–1 tank project instead of American builders. A U.S. machine tool firm, Cincinnati Milacron, however, won two big contracts on the XM–1 tank, but along with the Carlton Machine Tool Company its bid was rejected on the equipment required to construct the turret. Apparently, Carlton supplied the lowest bid after Mitsubishi on the equipment needed for the tank's turret, and partially for this reason Chrysler rejected its bid. An official at Chrysler provided two reasons for the selection of Mitsubishi. The first was the technological superiority of Mitsubishi's equipment; and the second was the lower price of the foreign tools, in spite of the advantages provided to Carlton from the Buy American Act. Carlton claimed that Mitsubishi's lower price resulted from possible dumping, and that what would eventuate from letting this contract to foreign builders would be the loss of U.S. jobs and the transfer of national security technology to overseas producers. Then Secretary of Defense Brown flatly rejected Carlton's assertions that the awarding of the contract to Mitsubishi would endanger national security technology.[55]

While rumors were still circulating concerning Chrysler's probable award of the turret XM–1 tank contract to foreign builders, the NMTBA had already begun to publicize what it considered to be the unfairness of the deal. In a statement delivered in November of 1977 to a Congressional Subcommittee on Trade concerned with U.S. antidumping regulations, the NMTBA sup-

---

*The X stands for experimental and has since been dropped from the tank's name; the official name now is the M–1Abrams tank. Chrysler Corporation—having experienced grave financial problems in 1979—no longer is the prime contractor of the M–1 tank. Two of the major builders of this tank today are General Dynamics and General Motors' Detroit Allison Division.

ported a bill which would prohibit the use of public funds to purchase foreign products "at less than fair value prices."[56] The NMTBA cited the not yet official Chrysler deal with Mitsubishi (though not by name) as an example of a case where the use of public funds would export American jobs abroad, while at the same time endangering national security technology.[57] Four months later in a statement presented to a Senate Subcommittee on International Finance, the NMTBA connected the Chrysler-Mitsubishi contract to the loss of revenues which could be utilized for U.S. machine tool research and development.[58]

The Carlton Machine Tool Company eventually sued Chrysler, Mitsubishi, and the Android Corporation for damages.[59] For its part, the NMTBA, apparently realizing its inability to hamstring the Department of Defense on its own, supported a circulated petition (that by the end of March of 1978 had some eighty congressional signatories on it) that attempted to prevent the use of Pentagon funds and U.S. tax dollars on foreign machine tool equipment. Unfortunately for the NMTBA and the Carlton Machine Tool Company, by April of 1978 both the Department of Defense and Chrysler made it known that work had begun on the XM–1 tank project according to the conditions specified in the contracts.[60]

As the technological competencies of foreign machine tool builders increase while their products become more price-attractive, the job of successfully applying political pressure on Washington bureaucrats becomes more difficult. This is especially true when an administration, such as the present one, espouses a free-market philosophy.

Consider the following issue. In May of 1984 GM's Fisher Body Division ordered a total of twenty-one highly automated press systems for automobile production. Two Japanese companies received orders for fifteen of these systems; a West German firm received two other orders. The four remaining orders went to the Danby Machine Corporation in Chicago. Actually, one Japanese manufacturer was the lowest bidder on all of the systems. However, GM's Fisher Body Division decided to distribute the orders to four different companies to expedite deliveries. Perhaps the NMTBA was acting out of this type of frustration in

June of 1984 when it urged the Reagan administration to take action on an NMTBA request to restrict imports through the use of a quota system.[61]

CONCLUSION

This chapter has analyzed the politics of the U.S. machine tool industry, which has been represented by the NMTBA. Some very important matters of great concern to the machine tool industry have been examined in this chapter. However, this is not to say that the NMTBA has not been active in other matters, such as attempting to mitigate the problem of product liability for builders.[62]

In spite of both its successes and failures, the NMTBA has been functioning as a very valuable, if not indispensable, political organization for U.S. machine tool builders. For some time now, the NMTBA has struggled to achieve the conditions and policies best suited for the U.S. machine tool industry. Given the many straits tool builders have been experiencing over the years both domestically and internationally, the NMTBA by necessity has had to gear its formalized interest group policies toward efforts to politically ameliorate conditions for the U.S. machine tool industry. What has directly resulted from these NMTBA efforts has been the crystalization of a protectionist posture, along with ongoing political attempts to both improve U.S. machine tool exports and liberalize the capital recovery system.

NOTES

1. Seymour Melman, *Our Depleted Society* (New York: Dell Publishing Co., Inc., 1965), pp. 52–53.

2. See "The 12th American Machinist Inventory of Metalworking Equipment 1976–1978," *American Machinist*, December 1978, p. 135; "The 13th American Machinist Inventory of Metalworking Equipment 1983," *American Machinist*, November 1983, p. 115.

3. See "Army Wars on Obsolescence," *American Machinist*, April 24, 1967, pp. 103–05.

4. Calculated from "The 13th American Machinist Inventory of Metalworking Equipment," *American Machinist*, November 1983, p. 115.

5. Quoted in "Machine Tool Imports vs. Exports," *Automotive Industries*, March 1, 1968, p. 77.

6. NMTBA Statement, June 4, 1970; see also "Machine Tool Industry Seeks Relief from Imports," *Industry Week*, June 15, 1970, p. 18.

7. "Statement of the National Machine Tool Builders' Association," presented to the *Committee on Ways and Means, Subcommittee on Trade Oversight Hearings on the Antidumping Laws*, November 21, 1977 (hereafter, NMTBA Statement, November 21, 1977).

8. "According to Article VII of GATT [General Agreement on Tariffs and Trade], dumping is defined as the sale of a product abroad at a lower price than is charged domestically." See Melvin B. Krauss, *The New Protectionism* (New York: New York University Press, 1978), p. 70. Krauss, who produced this book for the International Center for Economic Policy Studies, goes on to point out the following (pp. 70–71): "The truth of the matter is that predatory dumping by foreigners in the American market is much less of a problem than predatory protectionists who use alleged dumping by foreigners as an excuse to obtain protection in the domestic market."

9. Yet obviously all U.S. machine tool producers do not agree that Japanese builders have been dumping their products in the American market. A top official of a big U.S. machine tool company, Giddings & Lewis, Inc., remarked that because Japanese delivery times were down "they're price gouging." (This quote is from a questionnaire sent to Giddings & Lewis, Inc.)

10. See "Machine Tool Competition Toughens Here and Abroad," *Iron Age*, August 27, 1979, p. 99.

11. U.S. Department of Commerce, *U.S. Industrial Outlook, 1984*, p. 20–2; and "Houdaille Import Petition is Rejected," *American Machinist*, June 1983, p. 27.

12. U.S. Department of Commerce, U.S. Industrial Outlook, 1983, p. 20–2; and "Baldrige Backs NMTBA on Import Relief," *American Machinist*, May 1984, p. 23.

13. "Houdaille Import Petition is Rejected," *American Machinist*, June 1983, p. 27.

14. NMTBA Statement, November 21, 1977.

15. See, for example, "Machine Tool Builders Seek Government Protection," *Iron Age*, February 15, 1968, p. 97; and NMTBA Statement, June 4, 1970. (An example of a nontariff trade barrier is a border tax levied by a foreign government.)

16. See "Hokum Cocom," *The Economist*, March 8, 1975, p. 89.

17. "Statement of James A. Gray, Executive Vice President, National Machine Tool Builders' Association," made during *Hearings before the*

Subcommittee on International Finance of the Committee on Banking, Housing and Urban Affairs, United States Senate, March 23, 1976 (hereafter, NMTBA Statement, March 23, 1976).

18. Though the NMTBA has claimed that foreign machine tool builders have taken advantage of the much more restrictive interpretation of COCOM regulations in the U.S. since they have still been exporting their advanced machinery to the communist countries, the NMTBA nevertheless has conceded that "we have found it difficult to obtain specific documentation." See Ibid.

19. See, for example, "Testimony by National Machine Tool Builders' Association" before the *Subcommittee on International Economic Policy and Trade, Committee on International Relations*, House of Representatives, October 4, 1978 (hereafter, NMTBA Statement, October 4, 1978).

20. "Statement of Edward J. Loeffler, Technical Director, National Machine Tool Builders' Assocation," made during the *Hearings before the Subcommittee on International Economic Policy and Trade of the Committee on International Relations*, House of Representatives, June 14, 1978 (hereafter, NMTBA Statement, June 14, 1978).

. 21. NMTBA Statement, October 4, 1978.

22. Quoted in "Machine Tool Export Fate Rests on Capitol Hill," *Iron Age*, August 27, 1979, p. 48.

23. See Gray, "Machine Tool Exports: A Smaller Slice of a Bigger Pie," p. 10.

24. Data from the NMTBA, *1978–1979 Handbook*, p. 207. The figures for the years 1965, 1969, and 1975 are the Eastern Bloc's machine tool imports from the U.S.; for a list of the communist countries included in the Eastern Bloc, see Table 16.

25. See, for example, "Why World Trade Problems are Everybody's Problem—or Will Be Soon,'; *Iron Age*, January 2, 1978, p. 74.

26. "Statement by Ralph E. Cross, President, Cross Co., First Vice President National Machine Tool Builders' Association. Accompanied by James A. Gray, Executive Vice President," made during the *Hearings before the Subcommittee on International Trade, Committee on Banking and Currency*, House of Representatives, April 29, 1974 (hereafter, NMTBA Statement, April 29, 1974).

27. "Statement by James A. Gray, President, National Machine Tool Builders' Association, for a Meeting with Secretary of Commerce Kreps on Export Policy," (not dated; hereafter, NMTBA Statement to Secretary of Commerce Kreps on Export Policy).

28. NMTBA Statement, April 29, 1974.

29. See, for example, NMTBA Statement to Secretary of Commerce Kreps on Export Policy.

30. The Soviet Union is one of the world's leading consumers of machine tools. See NMTBA, *1978–1979 Handbook*, p. 151 for the years 1976 and 1977. For the years 1982 and 1983, see NMTBA, *1984–1985 Handbook*, p. 163.

31. NMTBA Statement, June 14, 1978.

32. Ibid., p. 231. Though instituted in 1974, the Jackson-Vanik Amendment did not adversely affect U.S. machine tool exports to the Eastern Bloc in 1974 or 1975 due to long delivery times.

33. In 1975 less than 15% of the total dollar value of all U.S. machine tool exports went to the Eastern Bloc nations.

34. NMTBA Statement, March 21, 1978.

35. See "Prepared Statement of James H. Mack," made in a *Hearing before the Technology Transfer Panel of the Committee on Armed Services*, House of Representatives, hearings held in June and July of 1983 (hereafter, NMTBA Statement, June and July 1983); and "Statement by James H. Mack, Public Affairs Director, National Machine Tool Builders' Association," made before the *Subcommittee on International Trade, Committee on Finance*, United States Senate, August 4, 1983 (hereafter, NMTBA Statement, August 4, 1983).

36. See NMTBA, *1984–1985 Handbook*, pp. 174–75.

37. NMTBA Statement, April, 29, 1974.

38. See NMTBA Statement, August 4, 1983. Also important to U.S. machine tool builders was the following major provision of the Export Administration Act of 1979. "In accordance with the provisions of this Act, the President shall not impose export controls for foreign policy or national security purposes on the export from the United States of goods or technology which he determines are available without restriction from sources outside of the United States in significant quantities and comparable in quality to those produced in the United States, unless the President determines that adequate evidence has been presented to him demonstrating that the absence of such controls would prove detrimental to the foreign policy or national security of the United States." However, this did not mean that both the Secretaries of Commerce and Defense would not maintain lists of items that could not be exported from the U.S. See *U.S. Code Congressional & Administrative News* (St. Paul, Minnesota: West Publishing Company, October, 1979).

39. See NMTBA Statement, June and July 1983; and NMTBA Statement, August 4, 1983.

40. See, for example, "Machine Tool Imports vs. Exports," *Automotive Industries*, March 1, 1968; and NMTBA Statement, June 4, 1970.

41. See "Statement of Ralph E. Cross, President, National Machine Tool Builders' Association," made during *Public Hearings before the Com-*

mittee on Ways and Means, House of Representatives, July 29, 1975 (hereafter, NMTBA Statement, July 29, 1975); and "Statement of J. B. Perkins, President, Hill Acme Company, Cleveland, Ohio, Accompanied by James A. Gray, Executive Vice President, National Machine Tool Builders' Association, and James H. Mack, Public Affairs Director, NMTBA," made during *Hearings before the Committee on Finance,* United States Senate, March 31, 1976 (hereafter NMTBA Statement, March 31, 1976).

42. "Statement of John E. Barbier, President, National Machine Tool Builders' Association, Accompanied by James A. Gray, Executive Vice President, and John Ellicott, Counsel," made in a *Public Hearing before the Committee on Ways and Means,* House of Representatives, March 15, 1973 (hereafter NMTBA Statement, March 15, 1973).

43. Quoted in "Corrective Action for the Machine Tool Squeeze," *Manufacturing Engineering,* August 1967, p. 24.

44. See NMTBA, *1978–1979 Handbook,* pp. 54–55.

45. See NMTBA Statement, March 15, 1973: "Statement of Joel Barlow, Counsel, National Machine Tool Builders' Association and American Machine Tool Distributors' Association," made during *Hearings before the Committee on Finance,* United States Senate, October 14, 1971 (hereafter, NMTBA Statement, October 14, 1971).

46. Cf. with the critical comment made by Congressman Vanik in NMTBA Statement, March 15, 1973.

47. Rather than abandon its argument, the NMTBA claimed that the reason domestic new orders of machine tools began declining in 1974, despite the existence of both the 7% investment tax credit and the Asset Depreciation Range System, was primarily because of the effects of price controls (which worsened the recession), high interest rates, and inflation. In short, according to the NMTBA, businesses simply ran out of capital. But this is somewhat questionable since after-tax corporate profits in 1974 increased by about $10 billion from the previous year. In any case, in January of 1975, the government increased the investment tax credit to 10% and the NMTBA indicated that domestic new orders of machine tools responded favorably to the improved tax credit system during the second quarter of that year. Though domestic new orders of machine tools continued to (slowly) increase in both the third and fourth quarters of 1975, as pointed out in the text, the entire year's domestic business was literally abominable. For the NMTBA's remarks, see NMTBA Statement, July 29, 1975; and NMTBA Statement, March 31, 1976.

48. In 1973, the wholesale price index for machine tools was 129.6; by 1974 it increased to 153.9, and in 1975 it rose to 180.5. See NMTBA, *1978–1979 Handbook,* p. 37.

49. Perry D. Quick, "Businesses: Reagan's Industrial Policy," *The Reagan Record*, eds. John L. Palmer and Isabel V. Sawhill (Cambridge, Massachusetts: Ballinger Publishing Company, 1984), p. 297.

50. See NMTBA, *1984–1985 Handbook*, p. 56.

51. Quoted in "The Bottom Could Drop Out of Capital Goods," *Business Week*, December 3, 1984, p. 137.

52. See, for example, NMTBA Statement, March 15, 1973; and NMTBA Statement, October 14, 1971.

53. NMTBA Statement, October 14, 1971. The NMTBA spokesman was referring to the employment reached in the machine tool industry in 1966. However, the machine tool industry did not employ 118,000 workers in 1966. In fact, in 1967 the machine tool industry actually employed more workers (116,400) than it did in 1966 (108,174). See NMTBA, *1978–1979 Handbook*, p. 211.

54. See NMTBA Statement to Secretary of Commerce Kreps on Capital Cost Recovery.

55. See "Chrysler Awards to Mitsubishi XM–1 Tooling Pact," *American Metal Market*, January 9, 1978, p. 1; and "Chrysler Tank Subcontract Causes Concern," *Iron Age*, April 17, 1978, pp. 30–32.

56. NMTBA Statement, November 21, 1977.

57. Ibid.

58. NMTBA Statement, March 21, 1978.

59. See "Carlton Sues Over Machine Center Pact," *American Metal Market*, June 12, 1978, p. 8.

60. See NMTBA Statement, March 21, 1978; and "Chrysler Tank Subcontract Causes Concern," *Iron Age*, April 17, 1978, p. 32.

61. "Machine Tool Orders Doubled from Year Ago," *The Wall Street Journal*, June 25, 1984, p. 5.

62. See "Statement on the National Machine Tool Builders' Association," before the *Subcommittee on Labor, Committee on Human Resources*, United States Senate, September 22, 1978.

6

Perspectives on Position

This concluding chapter serves three specific purposes: (1) it provides a general summary of the connections between advancing defense apparatus and machine tool business in the U.S.; (2) it explains how the problems of the American machine tool industry have infected manufacturing industries in the country and the entire society; and (3) it looks at what is probably in store for the industry in the remaining years of the 1980s, given current government policy.

A strong machine tool industry means a healthy industrial society. But one that has been experiencing rather profound problems will pass at least some of its troubles along to the nation. With military spending having had injurious effects on the U.S. machine tool industry during most of the postwar years, the country has had to pay the price to some degree.

MILITARY EXPENDITURES AND THE MACHINE TOOL INDUSTRY: A COMPENDIUM

This work has made clear that for many years arms production for the government and machine tool building in the U.S. have been closely related. Of course, it is true today, as it was in the past, that machine tool demand has been stimulated other than by weapons production. Such products as the sewing machine, the bicycle, the automobile, civilian aircraft, and others far too numerous to list have all directly contributed to machine tool business. But what is decisive to note here is that the continued development of a defense apparatus in the U.S. evolved into a lasting collision with the machine tool industry after the Second

World War. What historically had been more or less an occasional governmental stimulant to tool builders, in short, after World War II developed into a fetter; that is, a sustained military system in conjunction with the usage of defense spending as an economic regulatory instrument by the state have hindered the machine tool industry's growth process, while the progress of its major foreign competitors has continued more or less unabated. In Chapter 3 we have listed and discussed the structural problems of the American machine tool industry. Indeed, as we have seen the American machine tool industry has experienced damaging and critical problems in a number of areas, ranging from variable sales and profits to the import-export predicament. Each of the problems of the American machine tool industry can be traced to its ill-fated experience with the domestic business cycle. As Chapter 4 has made very plain, fluctuating military procurement contracts throughout most of the postwar period closely corresponded with domestic machine tool demand, as they did with the business cycle. Thus we can conclude here that since fluctuating military expenditures had been highly correlated with, and had a significant impact on, the very cyclical business of the machine tool industry, they likewise had been an important and contributing factor leading to the industry's other problems—problems which are very evident today.

But as this work has also indicated, the very defensive posture of the state apparatus in the U.S. throughout most of the postwar years has been problematic for the machine tool industry in yet another decisive way. Besides being related to the machine tool industry's very close relationship to the business cycle for a very considerable period, to varying degrees, all of the problems of builders discussed in Chapter 3 have also been adversely affected by the postwar allocation of a large amount of federal R&D expenditures for military purposes. The misapplication of much of the federal government's R&D resources has meant that the U.S. machine tool industry has been deprived of state subsidies that would have increased its technical competence, its productivity, and its overall industrial strength; all of this would have helped to make imports less attractive and U.S. machine tools more competitive in the world market. In short, for a number of years the machine tool industry has been exposed to a government apparatus which has found military spending to be most suitable to its domestic and global activities. It is precisely this type of government apparatus that has worked against the U.S. machine tool industry.

While the U.S. machine tool industry has had to contend with the deleterious effects of a permanent war economy and a generally uncooperative state policy that has sporadically varied defense expenditures, many foreign builders, most notably those in West Germany and Japan, have experienced a nonmilitary and technologically cooperative relationship with their governments. As a result, foreign machine tool builders have increasingly become more threatening to U.S. producers both at home and in the world market. Particularly interesting is the case of Japan. Twenty years or so ago the phrase "Made in Japan" to an American denoted ridicule for Japanese products—indeed the expression was synonymous with trifling items. Today the Japanese are the producers of high-quality goods and high-technology equipment, including machine tools of all different types. Moreover, today it is the Japanese machine tool builders who export more to the U.S. than producers in any other foreign nation.

Ironically enough, it was mainly the U.S. after World War II that built up the Axis Countries of Japan, West Germany, and, of course, Italy. "And now that we have changed their military defeat into economic success," as one U.S. machine tool builder expressed it in a speech concerned with the foreign competition, "we are again faced with aggression, economic aggression this time, but no less potentially deadly to us if we remain blindfolded."[1] However, the chances that the U.S. leaders will really remove their blindfolds are certainly not very good at all, since this would entail their significantly reducing the military apparatus.

Since the supersession of Keynesianism in the beginning of this decade, increasing military spending has been mainly limited to having immediate stimulating effects on machine tool demand, as indicated in Chapter 4. More money spent on defense means more machine tools, which seems to be very good for the industry. In fact, a recent study on the machine tool industry takes a similar position. The claim of this study is that machine tool technologies can be advanced and developed due to the large total impact of military spending on this industry.[2]

As we have seen, while there have been some benefits accruing to the machine tool industry (in regard to greater demand and technological spinoffs) because of defense spending, such a national-industrial policy is of limited significance. Indeed there is a major drawback. The growth of federal R&D expenditures for defense—from 61% of total government R&D funds in 1980 to 74% in 1983—is an ill omen for high-technology industries in an increasingly competitive world market. In the 1980s federally financed R&D spending for defense and related purposes as percentage of total R&D outlays for the nation has been steadily moving upward.[3]

In this day and age, and even more as time progresses, the nations that possess the most sophisticated civilian technologies are the ones that are most secure in the world markets. Focusing on military technologies means less attention given to civilian technologies. When a nation spends more than a third of its total R&D resources for defense and related purposes, the civilian sector must be at a disadvantage if some other advanced countries are simultaneously placing more emphasis on civilian industrial policies. Spending for military superiority and "star wars" technologies is not the same, by any stretch of the imagination, as spending specifically for the technological improvement of an industry. The measured efficacy of a national-industrial policy is a long-term determination. In respect to foreign machine tool industries, the civilian-industrial policies of West Germany and Japan have proven to be more efficacious in the long run. For example, the fact that Japanese and West German builders lead U.S. producers in the two important categories of "share of world exports" and "share of world output" is indicative of their proficiencies in both technical and standard tool making, and likewise suggests the effectiveness of industrial policies in these nations.

The Japanese in particular present a clear threat now and in the future to American industries, including the weakening machine tool industry. Noting that Japan is not a centrally planned society nor one where the government owns a large number of manufacturing companies, the president's Council of Economic

Advisors nevertheless recognizes the competitive strength of the Japanese. As the council states: "Some targeted industries, including semiconductors and machine tools, are almost certainly stronger than they would have been without government support and can be claimed as successes for Japanese industrial policy."[4] The success of the Japanese machine tool industry has in large part been due to subsidized R&D programs and tax incentives for innovative technological endeavors.

In marked contrast, the success story of the U.S. government has been the defense sector, where highly advanced war technologies have constantly been introduced in the postwar years. A major reason for much of the damage to the machine tool industry has been the relative technological depletion of this industry in recent years; nonetheless, continued high levels of defense spending remain a critical hurdle for U.S. builders. Thus as long as military spending remains a national priority in the U.S., high-technology competition will be difficult to overcome.

One final point should be made concerning how an enduring military policy has harmed the U.S. machine tool industry. In the area of export controls, excessive concentration on maintaining a massive defense apparatus has not been favorable to U.S. machine tool builders. Indeed, due to this apparatus machine tool exports to the communist countries have been reduced somewhat.

THE U.S. AND MACHINE TOOLS

It was World War II that struck the match that set industries ablaze throughout the country. America's superior industrial strength stemmed in large part from the condition of the nation's machinery. The war left America with a very large quantity of young and productive machine tools. It should be recalled that machine tools lie at the foundation of a country's industrial strength. "Machine tools often have been referred to as the 'machines which make machines." They are used both directly and indirectly in the production of all manufactured industrial products, consumer goods, and consumer services."[5] With nearly two-thirds of the nation's machine tools less than a decade old at the end of the Second World War, the stage was set for a period of prosperity since much of America's productive machinery was young and capable of the kind of output that leads to industrial growth.

America did prosper during the fifties and much of the sixties. However, during its period of prosperity metalworking users almost without interruption purchased fewer new machine tools. By 1963, as a result of the steady decline of young machine tools in use in the country since their peak in 1945, only 36% of the nation's metalcutting tools were under ten years of age. Between 1963 and 1968 the percentage of metalcutting machine tools less than ten years old increased to 37%, while the far less numerous metalforming machine tools continued their downward trend.[6] Conventional wisdom attributes this very slight increase in young metalcutting equipment in the nation solely to the institution of the 7% investment tax credit in the early sixties.[7] In other words, even before its formal merge to popularity, supply-side economics received the backing of business advocates. A government incentive like the institution of the investment tax credit, which reduces business tax liability and, in effect, operates as a direct business subsidy,[8] has traditionally been viewed as a legitimate form of state intervention. Unfortunately, this and similar types of incentives have been seen by the U.S. government as the sufficient condition for business advancement and increased market competitiveness at the same time technological proficiency has become more and more important.

While it is probably true that the investment tax credit stimulated machine tool demand to some extent during the 1963–1968 period, there is definitive evidence which unequivocally indicates that there is an additional matter which must be considered in respect to the increase in metalcutting tools at this time.

As already indicated in Chapter 4, the country's involvement in the imperial war in Vietnam greatly stimulated machine tool demand, with the really big increase coming during the early years of the conflict. Though it is virtually impossible to specify exactly how much new machine tool demand was stimulated by defense spending at this time, it is indisputable, just from the government's own increased purchasing of metalworking equipment, that the institution of the 7% investment tax credit was clearly not alone in accounting for the small growth in the percentage of young metalcutting tools during the years 1963–1968. Indeed, it seems far more credible that the Vietnam War accounted for a larger portion of the increase than did the investment tax credit. For example, in what was during the period 1963–1968 the largest fiscal year of the Department of Defense's direct procurement of machine tools, 1966, a total of $79,962,000 worth of metalcutting tools were purchased, compared to only $14,070,000 for metalforming tools. For metalcutting machine tools, this represented an increase over the preceding fiscal year of $43,058,000, while for metalforming equipment there was a growth of only $11,031,000. The tremendous gap between the Department of Defense's purchasing of a much larger dollar volume of metalcutting tools relative to metalforming tools continued in both fiscal years 1967 and 1968. Defense procurement of metalcutting tools exceeded metalforming equipment by more than five times in fiscal year 1967, and in fiscal year 1968 by better than eight times.[9] By also incorporating the indirect effects of defense spending on metalworking business at this time, it would therefore seem that the introduction of the 7% investment tax credit was a less important factor than military expenditures resulting from the Vietnam War in accounting for the small increase in metalcutting tools between 1963 and 1968.

This small but nonetheless real increase in the percentage of young metalcutting machine tools was not indicative of a changing pattern in metalworking purchases by American users. For by 1973, the *American Machinist* reported that the percentage of machine tools in the nation less than ten years of age had declined once again. This time not only had the percentage of metalforming machine tools decreased, but so also did metalcutting equipment. In fact, the percentage of young metalcutting machine tools in the country by 1973 had fallen to a level 3% lower than the one reached in 1963.[10] (There is another interesting point that should be made here. The fact that the percentage of young machine tools declined in 1973 casts further doubt on the investment tax argument cited in Chapter 5. That is, following the misplaced logic of this argument, the percentage of young machine tools in the country should have increased by 1973 since America's capital recovery system had improved somewhat by this time.) By the latter part of the 1970s the percentage of all machine tools less than a decade old became even smaller.

In 1983 metalcutting machine tools under ten years of age increased 3% to 34%; however, young metalforming tools continued to decline.[11] What accounted for this turnaround? Do the tax breaks granted to business in 1981 fully explain this increase in young metalcutting tools? It is hardly likely. Other things accounted for most of this increase in young metalcutting tools.

Metalcutting tools over twenty years old rose steadily for almost two decades, from the late 1950s to the late 1970s. Clearly, at some point at least a small portion of these old machine tools had to be replaced by users. In the latter part of the 1970s, prior to the 1981 tax changes, domestic new orders for metalcutting machine tools were increasing very sharply, due to economic expansion. This trend continued into 1980. Unquestionably this surge in the demand during the 1978–1980 period partly explains the increase in metalcutting machine tools in the 1983 survey.

Additionally, the recessions of 1980 and 1981–1982 generated a very noticeable slowdown in the growth of machine tool prices. (See Chapter 3, footnote 59.) So even though metalcutting orders slumped in the early 1980s, the very sharp decline in the growth of machine tool prices probably meant that more tools were purchased at this time than otherwise would have been the case. Significantly, as the economy was recovering the growth of machine tool prices was minimal. The marked slowdown of machine tool prices in the early 1980s may have been especially appealing to smaller manufacturers, prodding them to take advantage of this most exceptional period.[12]

Still another important factor accounting for this small increase in metalcutting machine tools was the very rapid growth of military spending. The need for machine tools in weapons production has already been unambiguously established in this work. But just to make the argument incontrovertible, military contract awards for metalcutting machine tools increased by over 200% from 1977 to 1983. In short, tax incentives played a minor role, at best, in the recent replacement of some metalcutting machine tools. Just as important is the fact that too few young machine tools are in users' establishments.

INFLATION AND PRODUCTIVITY

Of utmost importance is the question of what this large stock of old machine tools over the years has meant for the nation. With machine tools being as important as they are for an industrial society, it is not very hard to see that the manufacturing proficiency experienced when there is a young stock of metalworking equipment will gradually wane as this machinery grows older. In this respect, it is true that older, less productive machine tools helped to produce and sustain problems disastrous to the entire society.

There have been essentially two major problems related to the aged machine tools found in industries throughout the nation. The first of these problems is inflation, which, unlike recessions that really only affect some, has an impact on every person, institution, and industry in the society. A second major problem closely linked to obsolete machine tools is the nation's productivity problem. The point here is as follows: more younger machine tools mean increased production, and the latter provides the wherewithal to fight inflation.

Though there are a number of sources of inflation, helping to keep it under some sort of control in the past was the growing productivity of U.S. workers. The wage compensation businesses yielded to their employees was offset to some extent by increased productivity. Since productivity gains not infrequently more than compensated for the increased wages of workers, a potentially contributing source of inflation was held at bay. It was not, in other words, that workers did not demand and at times receive increases in their wages in the past, but rather with the aid of younger machine tools in the nation, productivity gains were instrumental and often sufficient both to meet workers' demands and to safeguard profits.

Table 17 empirically supports much of this argument. From 1960 to 1965 the annual percentage change in the hourly compensation provided to workers in the U.S. was smaller than the yearly percentage change in productivity (output per man-hour), except during the interval 1960–1961 where these changes were nearly identical. The direct result of this was that unit labor costs (obtained by dividing average hourly compensation by produc-

Table 17. Manufacturing Workers' Hourly Compensation, Manufacturing Productivity, and Producer Prices, 1960–1983

| | (Percentage Changes) | | |
Year	Hourly Compensation	Productivity	Producer Prices
1960	--	--	--
1961	3.0%	2.4%	-.4%
1962	4.0	4.7	.3
1963	3.2	7.0	-.3
1964	4.5	5.3	.2
1965	2.2	3.2	2.0
1966	4.7	1.1	3.3
1967	4.9	0	.2
1968	7.2	3.6	2.5
1969	6.9	1.7	3.9
1970	6.9	-.2	3.7
1971	6.1	6.1	3.2
1972	5.4	5.1	4.6
1973	7.1	5.4	13.1
1974	10.6	-2.4	18.9
1975	11.9	2.9	9.2
1976	8.1	4.4	4.6
1977	8.3	2.6	6.2
1978	8.3	.8	7.8
1979	9.7	.7	12.6
1980	11.7	.2	14.1
1981	9.9	3.5	9.2
1982	8.5	1.1	2.0
1983	5.4	6.2	1.3

Sources: Calculated from NMTBA, 1978-1979 Handbook, pp. 37 and 53; and NMTBA, 1984-1985 Handbook, pp. 41 and 55.

tivity) did not increase during the period 1960–1965. As can also be seen from Table 17, producers' prices were fairly stable from 1960 to 1965 (as were consumer prices which are not shown in the table). Between 1965 and 1982, the hourly compensation of workers increased faster than productivity in every year except 1971; this meant that unit labor costs were increasing during seventeen out of eighteen years in this period, and frequently quite rapidly.

In 1983 productivity increased by 6.2%, while hourly compensation in manufacturing grew by 5.4%. This reversal had an obvious effect on slowing down producer prices. But inflation actually slowed dramatically in 1982; at the same time, hourly compensation was increasing much faster than manufacturing productivity. In short, inflation slowed in the early 1980s because of recession, and the notable increase in productivity is currently proving to be cyclical—that is, ephemeral.

Productivity that has not exceeded workers' wages has left business with few major alternatives (in regard to prices) with which to deal with this problem domestically, apart from its traditional reliance on work speed-ups. One option would be to persistently refuse to grant wage increases. Selecting this option would mean that profits would not be diminished by wage increases; but, this option would create worker unrest and labor strikes amongst organized workers and yield a very high labor turnover rate among unorganized workers, since they would seek higher wages in those companies that pay more. A second alternative would be to yield occasionally to the wage demands of workers, because this would lessen the probability of worker dissatisfaction; yet, this selection would hurt business profits, since wages would be increasing faster than productivity. A third option would be for businesses to make periodic wage (and other) concessions to workers, while at the same time increase the prices of their products so as not to curtail their profits. Once businesses realize that what they are paying their employees is not being sufficiently offset by productivity gains, price increases to cover wage increases are inevitable, in addition to price increases to cover growing capital goods costs, such as those for raw materials.[13] That is, prices of merchandise will tend to rise since businesses will not just perfunctorily sit back and watch their profits diminish. Thus, for the most part, it has been the selection of this third option by manufacturing firms, a type of "cost-push inflation," that has made a significant contribution to rising prices in the U.S. from the mid–1960s to at least the beginning of this decade.

However, had businesses been adequately investing in new machine tools over the years, productivity clearly would have improved substantially, which would have had a dampening effect on inflation.[14] But businesses have not found this to be too practical for the most part due to rising machine tool prices. Making the matter even worse is that for a long period of time a number of machine tools had increased in price as fast or faster than wages.[15] This strongly suggests that businesses have utilized labor substitution in some cases instead of purchasing new machine tools (a matter to be discussed in more detail below).

There is no single cause for the productivity problem in the U.S. Indeed, there are a whole slew of reasons that have claimed to account for the nation's productivity problem. Some of these reasons have even been racist/sexist in design. Falling into this category have been the two reasons of women and minorities in the labor force. The argument here is that workers in these groups tend to be less experienced and skilled than white males. Other conventional explanations for the nation's productivity problem have been a young and relatively inexperienced work force; drug abuse; union demands; affirmative action; and the more popular notion of the oil crisis. Some supply-side reasons put forth in the past have been excessive government regulations and high business taxes, which supposedly were costly to companies since they diverted expenditures away from productive investments. Another has been the overutilization of Keynesian economic policies by the government. According to this supply-side explanation, the government gave too much attention to the regulation of demand and not enough to productivity.

Actually just what accounts primarily for the productivity slowdown in America is a very contentious issue. While some have blamed government "liberalism" others see declining work intensity as important. Of the many attempts to explain the productivity slowdown, and despite the varied political propensities, it seems difficult to dismiss superfluous military and related R&D spending.

Yet some have refused to accept the nation's commitment to military R&D as an important reason for the productivity problem. Even policy critics Gar Alperovitz and Jeff Faux, indicate that while military R&D spending has been harmful to the nation, by itself it is an inadequate explanation for the problem and it is not the most significant factor involved in the productivity slump.[16] Their argument is that between the mid–1960s and 1980 military R&D as a percentage of the national total declined while the country was experiencing a productivity problem.

But all this really tells us is that the productivity problem would have been worse if military R&D expenditures as a percentage of national output continued to grow or remained constant. It is precisely that the U.S. continued to allocate what was still a very large amount of R&D resources to the military, while many other industrial nations continued with their commitments to their civilian and commercial technologies, that is the issue. Over a period of, say, ten years this does make a difference.

Alperovitz and Faux note the large disparities between defense R&D as a percentage of national output in the U.S. compared to those in other industrial countries. But they fail to look at this in a comparative manner over a period of time.

Specifically, in 1965, as a percentage of gross domestic product, the U.S. spent about 6.5 times more than West Germany; in 1975 the U.S. was still spending about 4.7 times more than West Germany. The Japanese example is much more astonishing. As a percentage of gross domestic product, the U.S. devoted about seventy-five times more on military R&D than did the Japanese in 1965; by 1975 the U.S. was still spending almost sixty times more than the Japanese.[17] Significantly, in 1965 the U.S. was stepping up war efforts for the Vietnam conflict; in 1975 the U.S. was not involved in any war. Military expenditures, including defense R&D spending, understandably lost some, but by no means all, of their attractiveness to government officials during these years.

The critical point therefore is that the persistent misallocation

Chart 9. Graphic/Conceptual Relation of R&D to Productivity Growth

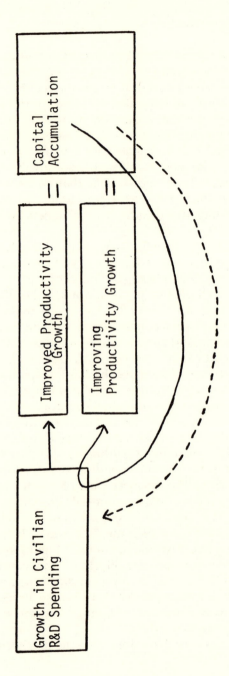

of the government's technological resources has a very negative influence on productivity, even if the significance of military and related R&D spending has declined, so long as other nations continue to devote their technological monies in the opposite direction. In competitive terms, the reduction (not the elimination) of something obviously damaging does not suggest that one's rivals, who have been far less infected, will not grow stronger if they continue to pursue a more rational industrial policy. Rather, what is suggested is that the strength of one's competitors disproportionately grows owing to overindulgence in technological misapplication. Whether or not this is the major factor that has damaged U.S. productivity growth is not the matter. What is the matter is that the disutility of defense R&D resources has been an important reason for the country's productivity problem.

Admittedly, increasing the concern, interest and enthusiasm of workers—in brief, more worker control and job security—will contribute to additional productivity growth. But increasing worker satisfaction while the nation spends heavily on wasteful and destructive technological projects at some point becomes tantamount to pushing on a string. Increased worker satisfaction ideally would be in concurrence with a rationally planned, state-directed R&D program. Rather than "radicalizing" the productive process, this would "humanize" it by making more efficient use of society's resources and workers.

In any case, the higher the expenditures for civilian R&D, the greater the potential for improving productivity. Thought of in a causal scheme, the movement is from R&D to increased productivity.[18] (See Chart 9.) Productivity will increase R&D expenditures only after it has generated sufficient economic growth to provide capital for technological investments. So if productivity is poor, there is a tendency for companies to neglect R&D expenditures, as much of the postwar period in the U.S. makes clear.

Also needed to be emphasized here is that the condition of the machine tool industry has been a very important factor contributing to the nation's productivity problem. As noted in detail in Chapter 3, the especially severe productivity problem within the U.S. machine tool industry, which has contributed very much to rising machine tool prices, has resulted from the negative impact of the business cycle on metalworking builders, which also reduces the capital available for R&D, and from the lack of technological assistance from the government for civilian purposes. Because the prices of U.S. machine tools have been on the increase, and through the years this has had the tendency to produce a do-not-buy-unless-absolutely-necessary attitude among metalworking users, as noted, too much old equipment has accumulated in the country. Incontrovertibly, old machine tools are not as productive as newer ones. As an official at General Motors correctly stated: "You can be as efficient as hell at doing something on equipment that's obsolete but you're not being productive."[19]

Old machine tools have therefore been an important and ongoing source of inflation (particularly pronounced in the past) and the productivity problem. These two major economic problems have clearly been exacerbated owing to the fact that postwar defense spending has injured the U.S. machine tool industry. These society-wide economic repercussions stemming from the machine tool industry can be understood more easily if one simply recalls how important this industry is to the overall industrial competence of the nation. Had the highly irrational decision of the government concerning the adoption of excessive defense spending not been made during the early postwar period, only to be annually reaffirmed thereafter with generally little opposition, it would certainly be true that the U.S. machine tool industry would have been in much better shape over the years, assuming that the state worked in a cooperative fashion with the civilian sector. A technologically stronger machine tool industry not experiencing a very critical and damaging productivity problem would have been able to stabilize the prices of its products, or at least prevent them from increasing too fast. Such a machine tool industry would have been able to protect itself from an import invasion, and also the metalworking equipment in the country would not have become aged during the postwar years.

A possible cause for concern presently is the total number of machine tools. Between 1978 and 1983 the total number of U.S. machine tools actually declined by 8%. Although the number of

numerical control tools doubled during this period—not surprising in a technological age—nonetheless, these machine tools
make up less than 5% of the total number of machine tools in
metalworking industries and only about 3.5% of the estimated
total in the U.S.[20]

LABOR SUBSTITUTION

Accompanying the penetrating economic troubles of inflation
and the productivity problem has been that many businesses
have had to make use of a compensating measure in order to
meet growing demand, due to their failure to adequately invest
in new metalworking equipment. This compensating measure
has been the increased use of labor. With the prices of some
machine tools rising as quickly as or even quicker than the wages
of workers, there has been a strong tendency at times for businesses to substitute labor for machine tools. Substituting labor
for new machine tools appears to have occurred especially frequently after the 1973–1975 recession. Faced with the high prices
of American-made machine tools, many metalworking users
found labor substitution, where possible, more economically appealing than purchasing new equipment, according to some au-
thorities. Businesses can simply increase the number of shifts
when sales improve rather than purchase new machine tools.
Once sales level off or decrease, the added shifts can be eliminated.[21] Less extreme although serving the same basic purpose
has been the use of overtime for workers which can similarly be
cut out when demand weakens. The point is that metalworking
users have turned to labor substitution periodically because when
their sales contract they apparently do not want to be stuck with
high-cost machine tools that they are unable to make sufficient
use of. The big problem is of course that labor substitution, while
somewhat effective in meeting increased demand, does not solve
the productivity problem.

While labor, and particularly *satisfied* labor, is an important
component of the productivity equation, it is still just the human
constituent part. From working with just crude hand tools, such
as those made from stone, wood, and animal bones and teeth,
man slowly but steadily developed more sophisticated forms of

hand tools like the hammer, wrench and pliers. With the appearance of machine tools a new, more productive element was
introduced into the work process. "Without machine tools,
everything would have to be made by hand. And, our standard
of living would be much as it was in the Civil War period ...
more than one-hundred years ago".[22] Clearly, as the technological means of production continuously advanced, so too did
productive output. In the present period it is unambiguously
clear that new machine tools, as decisive technological means
in the production process, generate increased output. In short,
it is the human element combined with and dependent upon
the stage of development of the technical component which will
account for what and how much is eventually produced in a
given period of time. Thus despite additional work shifts and
labor overtime, exactly what manufacturing employees produce
per hour worked (or productivity) relies in large part on new
machine tools.

Just as important is the fact that in the past the reliance of
some businesses on labor to meet their increased demand, though
meant to be a way in which costly investments for capital equipment could be averted, in the long run only accentuated inflation
in the country. Without sufficient productivity increases to offset
rising wages, as has been shown above, the inherent logic of
the system generally compels business to raise prices so as to
prevent any loss in their profits. But it would be unwarranted
optimism to suggest that the permanent rectification of the productivity problem in the U.S. could occur as long as the nation's
key capital-goods producing industry, the machine tool industry, is still troubled by defense spending. Undoubtedly a large
reduction in military spending would eventually strengthen the
U.S. machine industry, provided that the government made
efficient use of the nation's financial resources. This in time
would be favorable to many manufacturing industries. Yet presently there are no signs that would lead one to be optimistic.
Indeed, it is exceedingly difficult to give a full description of the
U.S. without spending a significant amount of time explaining
the massiveness of the American military apparatus and its global
scope.

THE PRESERVATION OF THE U.S. MACHINE TOOL INDUSTRY

If the machine tool industry can be considered the industrial lifeblood of the U.S., why, given its problems, have not many more of the bigger companies and conglomerates absorbed most of it?[23] If, for example, a company like General Motors, a very big metalworking user, were to buy out a machine tool firm (or two) it might appear that more capital would then become available for R&D, which in turn would be beneficial to machine tool productivity, prices, and international competitiveness. The immediate and direct benefit of buying out a machine tool firm for a company such as General Motors, it would seem, would be that its obsolete machine tools would be rapidly displaced and, concomitantly, its productivity would increase, thereby raising its profits. Thus it is possible to raise the argument that, excluding at this time machine tool firms themselves, metalworking consumers, especially the big ones, could at least somewhat reduce their economic woes were they to purchase machine tool companies.

There are major obstacles related to this matter, however, that need to be made clear. To begin with, we have previously noted in Chapter 3 that family ownership and control is a characteristic of the American machine tool industry. Big, small, and medium-sized tool firms tend to be controlled by family members. The sustaining of familial dominance within many machine tool companies in the U.S. has been accompanied by the traditional and sentimental values of builders connected with their business. These values have been buttressed by the so-called *art* of machine tool building which tends to connote the exclusiveness of this work. Despite the machine tool industry's problems, therefore, there is understandably a built-in reluctance on the part of many builders to sever the past and change the future. Moreover, it should be reemphasized here that machine tool companies have generally experienced good times when the economy is healthy, and so obviously this also has been a major reason—and a purely economic one—for their reluctance to sell out to larger companies.

From the side of the big machine tool users, one can also find very important reasons for their not having attempted to buy out machine tool companies to any large extent. Though machine tool companies usually do very well when the economy is strong, the opposite, as noted in an earlier chapter, occurs when the economy is weak. This indisputable characteristic of machine tool companies has made them unattractive to most metalworking users. Let us use the automobile industry as an example to convincingly demonstrate the major point to be made here. The automobile industry is a relatively cyclical industry. During good times automobile purchases increase and during bad times they decrease. Buying out machine tool companies, given the well-known and highly cyclical nature of machine tool sales, therefore, would not counteract the effect of a business downturn for automobile manufacturers. On the contrary, there would be an exacerbation of the slump. This inability of machine tool sales to counteract the business cycle has greatly contributed to making many metalworking users reluctant to absorb machine tool companies.

But increasing this reluctance among metalworking users has been another connected factor. The buying out of machine tool companies by metalworking users would in the long run not alter substantially the economic problems that have beset the machine tool industry. The business cycle would still severely and negatively affect machine tool building, despite whether it is being controlled by tool producing companies or by metalworking users, and so it would continue to create other related problems. For example, even if metalworking users made additional capital available for machine tool R&D they could do so only for a short period of time, or intermittently, since the harmful impact of the business cycle on tool production would continue to depress the accumulation of investment capital for technical purposes.

For both of these reasons, the purchasing of machine tool companies has not been viewed as economically practical by most metalworking users. Why should metalworking users buy the troubles of machine tool companies, especially when they are not easily solvable ones? Of great importance also is the fact that the absorbtion of machine tool companies by metalworking users would certainly not mean that government R&D expenditures would be forthcoming for civilian machine tool development. Finally, and not insignificantly, many metal-working consumers are unable to afford to buy out a machine tool business.

All of these above reasons together have prevented U.S. machine tool firms from being rapidly absorbed by metalworking users in the country. While machine tool companies have not entirely avoided acquisitions (the Bendix Corporation, for example, consolidated a number of tool producing firms),[24] most of the industry has remained independent of the majority of big metalworking users.

Given the industrial importance of machine tools, and noting that there has been no significant trend toward buying out tool producing companies by metalworking users due to the reluctance of both the former and the latter, it is nevertheless evident that at least some big consumers of machine tools have employed an alternative. This alternative is for big machine tool users to design and build the equipment they need themselves. An official at General Motors, for example, in 1976 asserted that "The machine tool industry has been relatively stagnant in its R&D" and that the equipment the company was purchasing was "the same we bought 25 or even 50 years ago, except maybe with some digital stuff hung on the side so they cost more."[25] The result was that General Motors, whose productivity had been negatively affected due to poor equipment, decided to design a new parts grinder machine capable of working much faster than comparable tools then in existence. Another example is the aerospace firm Rohr Industries, Inc. Rohr designed and built a large number of machine tools, while also receiving requests from other aerospace firms to construct metalworking equipment. Remarked a spokesman from Rohr in the late 1970s: "We don't think we're smarter than Kearney & Trecker or Cincinnati Milacron, but we do have the mechanical and electronic expertise to do it and we know our costs."[26] Thus the dissatisfaction of some big metalworking users with the U.S. machine tool industry has not prompted the absorbtion of tool producing firms; rather, these users have obviously found the utilization of their own technical manpower and resources to be more economically sensible and expedient. In other words, why buy a machine tool firm and acquire additional headaches when you can design and construct your own metalworking equipment?[27]

Exactly how widespread this trend is amongst metalworking users is unknown. Needless to say, if this trend were too pervasive the machine tool industry would virtually disappear due to a lack of business. Yet the major point is that if a company the size of General Motors, one of the leading industrial enterprises in the country, opted to design some of its own machine tools rather than absorb a machine tool firm, then it is fairly safe to maintain that the process of amalgamation to other metalworking consumers is not too appealing to them either.

FUTURE PROSPECTS: REVITALIZATION OR DECLINE

Much of what happens to the machine tool industry in the years ahead is contingent upon the policy direction of government. At the moment, the policy direction is biased heavily toward a free-market, noninterventionist philosophy by government. This philosophy, having its roots in the classical tradition, in recent years has been popularized by supply-side economics. In one very noticeable way, this new breed of noninterventionists has departed from the classical tradition. Whereas it was originally believed that an 'invisible hand" was the driving force of the economy, today this traditional idea has lost its significance. Champions of modern-day noninterventionism argue that capitalism, as a system of production, "is guided not by an invisible hand, but by the quite visible and aggressive hand of management and entrepreneurship."[28] Their goal: high profits. It is these high profits that supposedly induce innovative research and development.[29] The major problem of the economy: the government "wedge."[30] If government would recede from the economy, work incentives would improve and business would soon be on a high-profit path. The central dictum of this school of thought, which is clearly reflected in the present administration's policies, is that supply creates its own demand but "subsidized supply destroys demand."[31]

Thus we are instructed to push government out of our lives;

both society and economy would do far better without the shackles of government. Since its implementation, this policy has had as its ongoing goal the reduction in the size of government, apart from the Pentagon budget. Yet despite the strong emphasis on noninterventionism, the competitiveness of U.S. industry has not improved. Specifically, the competitiveness of the U.S. machine tool industry has, if anything, worsened in recent years.

There are, however, other proposed methods to the revitalization of U.S. industries. One such approach to increasing American competitiveness is more liberal in design than the free-market philosophy. Though this approach still views government as cumbersome, there is emphasis placed on what government can do to help American industries in an increasingly competitive environment. Accordingly, this approach, developed by the team from *Business Week*, argues that the "reindustrialization" of America requires, among other things, a government organization to direct money to industries in need.[32] The proponents of the reindustrialization approach maintain, though not too decisively, that the machine tool industry *"may* need government assistance to gain access to capital for expansion. Faster depreciation and more supportive export policies would help, and the fragmented industry might also benefit from further consolidation."[33]

More liberal and radical plans than that proffered by the *Business Week* group concerning the revitalization of American industries offer some very insightful ideas and suggestions.[34] All of these plans for industrial revitalization argue for a much-enlarged role for government, while some see the need for democratized participation. In short, it is widely perceived that the U.S. lacks and is in need of a targeted, planned, and *comprehensive* industrial policy. Indeed, the need for such a policy has even been recognized by some business people.

But the current administration has no real industrial policy. When business advocates declare that the "Reagan economic policy can be thought of as a weak form of reindustrialization,"[35] then one can be certain that a rationally planned program for industrial revitalization is not part of the policy agenda. Rather than revitalization of industry, the current program underscores rearmament.

Between fiscal years 1984 and 1988 the military budget currently is estimated to grow by more than 57%. Thus military spending will increase from 6.4% of the GNP to 7.3%. After accounting for inflation, real defense spending is expected to rise by about 34% during this same period; in contrast, real nondefense spending is estimated to grow by less than 1%.[36]

Military R&D spending (not including space R&D) is projected to grow by 82% between fiscal years 1984 and 1988. Thus defense R&D will grow from .64% of the GNP to .85% in the next few years.[37] The budget for fiscal year 1986 informs its readers that military R&D spending includes, among other things:

... an expanded effort on the administration's strategic defense initiative, a research program to explore the possibility of eliminating the ballistic missile threat to the United States and its allies. This initiative includes research on space surveillance and target acquisition; directed energy weapons; kinetic energy weapons; battle management systems; and system survivability.[38]

The current and planned enlargement of the defense budget and the accompanying high growth of military R&D earmarked largely for sophisticated war technologies is egregiously wasteful and counterproductive for both industry and members of this society.

It is not the purpose nor the intention of this study to suggest a detailed industrial policy that will be advantageous to industry and, ultimately, to society. Such a reasonable policy is necessary but obviously nonexistent. The answer to the question of where the U.S. would get the funds necessary to enlarge its civilian technological endeavors would clearly be from the military. Indeed, meaningful reductions in the defense budget, even if only effected initially by siphoning off inflation-guarding excesses, could easily bring about the beginning of a rational civilian-directed industrial policy. Between fiscal years 1985 and 1988 a total of $23.5 billion could be saved by freezing *real* military spending at the 1985 level. Doing just this would provide nearly $6 billion for a civilian industrial policy in each of the four years covered during this period.

Freezing current military outlays at their 1985 level would save a total of $104.6 billion by fiscal year 1988. An actual retrenchment of the Pentagon's budget would provide the needed funds for a viable and effective industrial policy. Rather than devote more and more funds to the military for extraneous technology (e.g., the Trident II and the Peacekeeper missiles) in the future, these public monies could be very usefully spent on the furtherance of civilian technologies.

Unfortunately, the present gives us a good idea of what to expect in the immediate future. Budgetary priorities have already been set and defense spending has even more support today than it has had in the past. The commitment the government has made to advancing military spending at the present time precludes the development of a practical industrial policy in the immediate future. For this reason, the competitiveness of the U.S. machine tool industry will probably continue to deteriorate in the 1980s. A free-market philosophy and supply-side "incentives" will be incapable of repositioning the American machine tool industry.

NOTES

1. Quoted in "Machine Tool Competition Toughens Here and Abroad," *Iron Age*, August 27, 1979, p. 76.

2. See Committee, *The U.S. Machine Tool Industry*, p. 87.

3. See U.S. Bureau of the Census, *Statistical Abstract of The United States: 1984* (104th Edition), Washington, D.C., 1983, p. 593.

4. *Economic Report of the President* (Washington, D.C.: U.S. Government Printing Office, 1984), pp. 95–98.

5. See Willard J. McCarthy and Robert E. Smith, *Machine Tool Technology* (Bloomington, Illinois: McKnight & McKnight Publishing Co., 1968), p. 24.

6. See "The 11th American Machinist Inventory of Metalworking Equipment 1973," *American Machinist*, October 29, 1973, p. 143.

7. Ibid.

8. See The Business Week Team, *The Reindustrialization of America* (New York: McGraw-Hill Book Company, 1982), p. 125.

9. Data calculated from the Department of Defense, OASD (Comptroller), Directorate for Information Operations, *Military Prime Contract Awards by Service Category and Federal Supply Classification.*

10. See "The 11th American Machinist Inventory of Metalworking Equipment 1973," p. 143.

11. See "The 13th American Machinist Inventory of Metalworking Equipment 1983," *American Machinist*, November 1983, pp. 113–15.

12. See Ibid., p. 115, for a description of newer machine tools in smaller plants.

13. Cf. with Thomas Weisskopf, "Sources of Cyclical Downturns and Inflation," *The Capitalist System*, eds. Richard C. Edwards et al. (1978 edition), p. 452.

14. Cf. with James A. Gray, "Productivity: The Inflation Fighter," pp. 2–8. This was an address given by Gray to the members of the National Machine Tool Builders' Association on March 15, 1979.

15. See Melman, *The Permanent War Economy*, p. 82 and appendix 1. This point is also made in some of Melman's other works dealing with productivity and inflation. See, for example, "Decision Making and Productivity as Economic Variables: The Present Depression as a Failure of Productivity," *Journal of Economic Issues*, June 1976, p. 224; and "Inflation and Unemployment as Products of a War Economy: The Trade Union Stake in Economic Conversion" (a paper based on a speech given in 1976 to the United Electrical, Radio and Machine Workers of America), p. 7.

16. Gar Alperovitz and Jeff Faux, *Rebuilding America*, (New York: Pantheon Books, 1984), p. 92.

17. Calculated from Organization for Economic Co-operation and Development, *Technical Change and Economic Policy*, p. 40.

18. Cf. with Leonard, "Research and Development in Industrial Growth," pp. 232–56; cf. also with Thomas E. Weisskopf, Samuel Bowles and David M. Gordon, "Hearts and Minds: A Social Model of U.S. Productivity Growth," *Brookings Papers on Economic Activty*, 2:1983, eds. William C. Brainard and George L. Perry (Washington, D.C.: The Brookings Institute, 1984), pp. 381–441, but especially pp. 389–90.

19. Quoted in "How GM Manages its Billion-Dollar R&D Program," *Business Week*, June 28, 1976, p. 57.

20. See "The 13th American Machinist Inventory of Metalworking Equipment, 1983," pp. 113–19.

21. See *Production Engineering*, August 1978, p. 40.

22. National Machine Tool Builders' Association (booklet), *Machine Tools/Existing Careers in an Electronic Age*.

23. It should be noted that a few big U.S. companies—such as Litton Industries and Rockwell International—do have their own machine tool divisions.

24. The proposed union in early 1980 between Bendix and Warner & Swasey (see "Machine Tool Companies Grow Fewer and Bigger," *Iron Age*, January 21, 1980, pp. 23–26) occurred later that year.

25. Quoted in "How GM Manages its Billion-Dollar R&D Program," *Business Week*, June 28, 1976, p. 57.

26. Quoted in "Can U.S. Machine Tools Maintain an Edge?" *Industry Week*, August 21, 1978, p. 67.

27. See "Government: Machine-Tool Builders Warn ITC on Imports," *American Machinist*, August 1983, p. 21.

28. George Gilder, *Wealth and Poverty* (New York: Basic Books, Inc., 1981), p. 37.

29. Ibid.

30. For an elaboration of the supply-side "wedge" concept, see Jude Wanniski, *The Way the World Works* (New York: Simon and Schuster/ Touchstone, 1979) pp. 84–85.

31. See Gilder, chapter 4.

32. The Business Week Team, *The Reindustrialization of America*, pp. 183–84.

33. Ibid., pp. 156–57. (Emphasis added).

34. See Magaziner and Reich, *Minding America's Business*; Alperovitz and Faux, *Rebuilding America*; and Samuel Bowles, David M. Gordon and Thomas E. Weisskopf, *Beyond the Waste Land: A Domocratic Alternative to Economic Decline* (New York: Anchor Press/Doubleday, 1983).

35. The Business Week Team, *The Reindustrialization of America*, p. 181.

36. Figures calculated from *The United States Budget in Brief, Fiscal Year 1986* (Washington, D.C.: U.S. Government Printing Office, 1985) pp. 65 and 77.

37. Figures calculated from Ibid., pp. 68 and 77.

38. *Budget of the United States Governemnt, Fiscal Year 1986* (Washington, D.C.: U.S. Government Printing Office, 1985), pp. 5–11.

Selected Bibliography

BOOKS, ARTICLES, AND REPORTS

Abert, James G. and Clayton McCuistion. *The Defense Dependency of the Metalworking Machinery and Equipment Industry and Disarmament Implications*. Bethesda, Maryland.: Resource Management Corporation, 1969.

Aerospace Industries Association of America, Inc. *Aerospace Facts and Figures, 1982/83*. New York: Aviation Week & Space Technology, 1982.

Alperovitz, Gar and Faux, Jeff. *Rebuilding America*. New York: Pantheon Books, 1984.

Armstrong, Arthur. "The Persistence of Struggle: The Story of the Acme-Cleveland Corporation," 1976 (an address given to the Newcomen Society).

Barnet, Richard J. *Roots of War*. New York: Atheneum, 1972.

Bowles, Samuel, David M. Gordon and Thomas E. Weisskopf. *Beyond the Wasteland: A Democratic Alternative to Economic Decline*. New York: Anchor Press/Doubleday, 1983.

Committee on the Machine Tool Industry, Manufacturing Studies Board, Commission on Engineering and Technical Systems, National Research Council. *The U.S. Machine Tool Industry and the Defense Industrial Base*. Washington, D.C.: National Academy Press, 1983.

Cypher, James. "Capitalist Planning and Military Expenditures." *The Review of Radical Political Economics*. Fall 1974, 1–19.

Floud, Roderick, *The British Machine Tool Industry*, 1850–1914. London: Cambridge University Press, 1976.

Gilder, George. *Wealth and Poverty*. New York: Basic Books, Inc., 1981.

Hollomon, J. Herbert. *Technical Change and American Enterprise*. Washington, D.C.: National Planning Association, 1974.

———. "Technology in the United States: Issues for the 1970s." *Technology Review*, June 1972, 10–21.

Hollomon, J. Herbert and Allan E. Harger. "America's Technological Dilemma." *Technology Review*, July/August 1971, 31–40.

Koistinen, Paul A. "The Industrial-Military Complex in Historical Perspective: The InterWar Years." *The Journal of American History*, March 1970, 819–39.

Krauss, Melvin B. *The New Protectionism*. New York: New York University Press, 1978.

Leonard, William N. "Research and Development in Industrial Growth." *Journal of Political Economy*, March/April 1971, 232–56.

McCarthy, William J. and Robert E. Smith. *Machine Tool Technology*. Bloomington, Illinois.: McKnight & Mcknight Publishing Company, 1968.

McDougall, Duncan M. "Machine Tool Output, 1861–1910." *Output, Employment, and Productivity in the United States after 1800, Studies in Income and Wealth*, Vol. 30, pp. 497–517. New York: National Bureau of Economic Research, 1966.

"Machine Tools," *Machinery's Encyclopedia*, IV. New York: Industrial Press, 1917, 278–83.

Magaziner, Ira C. and Robert B. Reich. *Minding America's Business*. New York: Harcourt Brace Jovanovich, Publishers, 1982.

Melman, Seymour. "Decision Making and Productivity as Economic Variables: The Present Depression as a Failure of Productivity." *Journal of Economic Issues*, June 1976, 218–40.

————. "Inflation and Unemployment as Products of a War Economy: The Trade Union Stake in Economic Conversion." (This paper is based upon a speech given in 1976 to the United Electrical, Radio and Machine Workers of America.)

————. *Our Depleted Society*. New York: Dell Publishing Co., Inc., 1965.

————. *Pentagon Capitalism*. New York: McGraw-Hill Book Company, 1970.

————. *The Permanent War Economy*. New York: Simon and Schuster, 1974.

Moody's Handbook of Common Stock. Fall 1984 ed. New York: Moody's Investory Service, Inc., 1984.

Noble, David F. "Social Choice in Machine Tool Design: The Case of Automatically Controlled Machine Tools." *Case Studies on the Labor Process*, ed. Andrew Zimbalist, pp. 18–50. New York: Monthly Review Press, Inc., 1979.

Organization for Co-operation and Development. *Patterns of Resources Devoted to Research and Experimental Development in the OECD Area, 1963–1971*. Paris: OECD, 1975.

————. *Technical Change and Economic Policy*. Paris: OECD, 1980.

————. *OECD Science and Technology Indications*, Paris: OECD, 1984.

Quick, Perry D. "Businesses: Reagan's Industrial Policy." *The Reagan Record*, eds. John L. Palmer and Isabel V. Sawhill, pp. 287–316. Cambridge, Massachusetts: Ballinger Publishing Company, 1984.

Reich, Michael. "Military Spending and Production for Profit." *The Capitalist System*, eds. Richard C. Edwards et al., pp. 409–17. Englewood Cliffs, New Jersey: Prentice-Hall, 1978.

Reich, Michael and David Finkelhor. "Capitalism and the Military-Industrial Complex." *The Capitalist System*, eds. Richard C. Edwards et al., pp. 392–406. Englewood Cliffs, N.J.: Prentice-Hall, 1972.

Roberts, Paul Craig. *The Supply-Side Revolution*. Cambridge, Massachusetts: Harvard University Press, 1984.

Robertson, Ross M. "Changing Production of Metalworking Machinery, 1860–1920." *Output, Employment, and Productivity in the United States after 1800, Studies in Income and Wealth*, Vol. 30, pp. 479–95. New York: National Bureau of Economic Research, 1966.

Rosenberg, Nathan. "Technological Change in the Machine Tool Industry, 1840–1910." *The Journal of Economic History*, December 1963, 414–43.

Rosenbloom, Richard. *Technology Transfer—Process and Policy: An Analysis of the Utilization of Technological By-Products of Military and Space R&D*. Washington, D.C.: National Planning Association, 1965.

Standard & Poors. *Industry Surveys, Machinery* (various issues).

Stoughton, Bradley. *History of the Tools Division, War Production Board*. New York: McGraw-Hill Book Company, Inc., 1949.

The Business Week Team. *The Reindustrialization of America*. New York: McGraw-Hill Book Company, 1982.

U.S. Code Congressional & Administrative News. St. Paul, Minnesota: West Publishing Company, October 1979.

Wagoner, Harless D. *The U.S. Machine Tool Industry from 1900–1950*. Cambridge, Massachusetts: The M.I.T. Press, 1968.

Wanniski, Jude. *The Way the World Works*. New York: Simon and Schuster/Touchstone, 1979.

Weisskopf, Thomas. "Sources of Cyclical Downturns and Inflation." *The Capitalist System*, eds. Richard C. Edwards et al., pp. 441–55. Englewood Cliffs, New Jersey.: Prentice-Hall, 1978.

Weisskopf, Thomas E., Samuel Bowles and David M. Gordon. "Hearts and Minds: A Social Model of U.S. Productivity Growth." *Brookings Papers on Economic Activity*, 2:1983, eds. William C. Brainard and George L. Perry, pp. 381–441. Washington, D.C.: The Brookings Institute, 1984.

Yarmolinsky, Adam. *The Military Establishment*, New York: Perennial Library, 1973.

York, Herbert J. and G. Allen Greb. "Military Research and Development: A Postwar History." *Bulletin of the Atomic Scientists*, January 1977, 13–26.

U.S. GOVERNMENT PUBLICATIONS

Budget of the United States Government, Fiscal Year 1986. Washington, D.C.: U.S. Government Printing Office, 1985.

Department of Defense, *100 Companies Receiving the Largest Dollar Volume of Prime Military Contracts* (annual).

———. OASD (Comptroller), Directorate for Information Operations, *Military Prime Contract Awards by Service Category and Federal Supply Classification*.

Economic Report of the President. Washington, D.C.: U.S. Government Printing Office, 1984.

Henry, David K. "Defense Spending: A Growth Market for Industry." In U.S. Department of Commerce, *U.S. Industrial Outlook, 1983*, XXXIX-XLVII.

Hintz, Otto E., James H. Sullivan, and Robert C. Van Parys. *Machine Tool Industry Study: Final Report*. Rock Island, Illinois.: U.S. Army Industrial Base Engineering Activity, November 1, 1978.

Historical Statistics of the United States, Colonial Times to 1970, Bicentennial Edition, Washington, D.C., 1975.

Joint Economic Committee of Congress. *Plugging in the Supply Side*. Washington, D.C.: U.S. Government Printing Office, 1980.

National Science Foundation. *Research and Development in Industry, 1975*. Washington, D.C., 1977.

The United States Budget in Brief, Fiscal Year 1986. Washington, D.C.: U.S. Government Printing Office, 1985.

U.S. Arms Control and Disarmament Agency. *World Military Expenditures and Arms Transfers, 1967–1976*. Washington, D.C.

U. S. Bureau of the Census. *1972 Census of Manufacturers*. Washington, D.C.

———. *1977 Census of Manufactures*. Washington, D.C.

———. *1982 Census of Manufactures* (preliminary reports on metalcutting and metalforming machine tools, July 1984). Washington, D.C.

———. *Statistical Abstract of the United States*: 1984 (104th edition). Washington, D.C. 1983.

U.S. Department of Commerce. *Business Conditions Digest* (December 1969, April 1983, and May 1984 issues).

———. *U.S. Industrial Outlook* (1968, 1974, 1979, 1983, and 1984 issues).

NATIONAL MACHINE TOOL BUILDERS' ASSOCIATION MATERIALS

Gray, James A. "Machine Tool Exports: A Smaller Slice of a Bigger Pie," September 19, 1979 (an address given to the Annual Forecasting Conference of the National Machine Tool Builders' Association).

———. "Productivity: The Inflation Fighter," March 15, 1979 (an address given to the members of the National Machine Tool Builders' Association).

National Machine Tool Builders' Association. *Directory 1979*. McLean, Virginia.: NMTBA, 1978.

———. *1978–1979 Economic Handbook of the Machine Tool Industry*. McLean, Virginia.: NMTBA, 1978.

———. *1984–1985 Economic Handbook of the Machine Tool Industry*. McLean, Virginia.: NMTBA, 1984.

——— (booklet), *Machine Tools/America's Muscles*.

——— (booklet). *Machine Tools/Basic to the Nation*.

——— (booklet). *Machine Tools/Existing Careers in an Electronic Age*.

——— (booklet). *Machine Tools/New Concepts for a New Day*.

"Prepared Statement of James H. Mack," made in a *Hearing before the Technology Transfer Panel of the Committee on Armed Services*, House of Representatives. Hearings held in June and July of 1983.

"Statement by Craig R. Smith, Second Vice Chariman, National Machine Tool Builders' Association, for a Meeting with Secretary of Commerce Kreps on Capital Cost Recovery" (not dated).

"Statement of Edward J. Loeffler, Technical Director, National Machine Tool Builders' Association," made during the *Hearings before the Subcommittee on International Economic Policy and Trade of the Committee on International Relations*, House of Representatives, June 14, 1978.

"Statement of James A. Gray, Executive Vice President, National Machine Tool Builders' Association," made during *Hearings before the Subcommittee on International Finance of the Committee on Banking, Housing and Urban Affairs*, United States Senate, March 23, 1976.

"Statement by James A. Gray, President, National Machine Tool Builders' Association, for a Meeting with Secretary of Commerce Kreps on Export Policy" (not dated).

"Statement of James A. Gray, President, National Machine Tool Builders' Association, McLean, Va., Accompanied by Kurt O. Tech, Group Vice President, The Cross Co., Fraser, Mich., and George J. Becker, President and Chief Executive Officer, Giddings &

Lewis, Inc., Fond Du Lac, Wis.," made during *Hearings before the Subcommittee on International Finance of the Committee on Banking, Housing and Urban Affairs*, United States Senate, March 21, 1978.

"Statement of James H. Mack, Public Affairs Director, National Machine Tool Builders' Association," made before the *Subcommittee on International Trade, Committee on Finance*, United States Senate, August 4, 1983.

"Statement of J.B. Perkins, President, Hill Acme Company, Cleveland, Ohio, Accompanied by James A. Gray, Executive Vice President, National Machine Tool Builders' Association, and James H. Mack, Public Affairs Director, NMTBA," made during *Hearings before the Committee on Finance*, United States Senate, March 31, 1976.

"Statement of Joel Barlow, Counsel, National Machine Tool Builders' Association and American Machine Tool Distributors' Association," made during *Hearings before the Committee on Finance*, United States Senate, October 14, 1971.

"Statement of John E. Barbier, President, National Machine Tool Builders' Association, Accompanied by James A. Gray, Executive Vice President, and John Ellicott, Counsel," made in a *Public Hearing before the Committee on Ways and Means*, House of Representatives, March 15, 1973.

"Statement of the National Machine Tool Builders' Association, Henry D. Sharpe, Jr., First Vice President," made during the *Hearing before the Committee on Ways and Means*, House of Representatives, June 4, 1970.

"Statement of the National Machine Tool Builders' Association," before the *Subcommittee on Labor, Committee on Human Resources*, United States Senate, September 22, 1978.

"Statement of the National Machine Tool Builders' Association," presented to the *Committee on Ways and Means, Subcommittee on Trade Oversight Hearings on the Antidumping Laws*, November 21, 1977.

"Statement by Ralph E. Cross, President, Cross Co., First Vice President, National Machine Tool Builders's Association, Accompanied by James A. Gray, Executive Vice President," made during the *Hearings before the Subcommittee on International Trade, Committee on Banking and Currency*, House of Representatives, April 29, 1974.

"Statement of Ralph E. Cross, President, National Machine Tool Builders' Association," made during *Public Hearings before the Committee on Ways and Means*, House of Representatives, July 29, 1975.

"Testimony by National Machine Tool Builders' Association," before the *Subcommittee on International Economic Policy and Trade, Committee on International Relations*, House of Representatives, October 4, 1978.

NEWSPAPERS, MAGAZINES, AND TRADE JOURNALS

American Machinist
American Metal Market
Automation
Automotive Industries
Business Week
The Economist
Fortune
Industry Week
Iron Age
Manufacturing Engineering
Mechanical Engineering
Production Engineering
Purchasing
The Wall Street Journal
The Wall Street Transcript

Index

Accelerated Cost Recovery System, 145, 147
Acme-Cleveland Corporation, 25, 44; R&D of, 51
Aerospace industry, 5, 44, 81, 95, 103, 105, 110; R&D in, 48, 57–60, 86 n.48,; military demand in, 96, 102–3, 105, 111–12
Aircraft industry, 27, 57, 103; military demand in, 24, 26, 28–31, 111. *See also* Aerospace industry
Air Force, 56–57
Alperovitz, Gar, 168–69
AMCA International Corporation, 119
American (U.S.) machine tool industry, 4–7, 9, 24–30, 32, 39–40, 46, 97, 106, 108–10, 113, 115, 157, 159, 161, 174; backlogs in, 66–71; capital recovery,142–47, 150; composition of, 40; economic concentration in, 42–43; effects of business cycle on, 6, 19, 23, 26–28, 32, 34, 44, 46–48, 50–51, 61, 80–82, 89–93, 98–99, 103, 110, 118–20, 127, 158, 171, 176; emergence of, 21; employment in, 40, 42–43, 72, 73, 146; expenditures for new plant and equipment in, 47–49, 80; exports, 74–76, 78–80, 118, 127, 131–42, 150; import problem, 56, 74–77, 79–80, 110, 113, 127–31, 145, 147, 172; international competitiveness of, 6, 47, 82, 158, 178, 180; inventories of, 68, 70; lead and delivery times in, 67–71, 79; preservation of, 174–77; productivity in, 6, 61–65, 67, 114, 158, 171; protectionism of, 127–31, 150; R&D in, 6, 48–61, 80, 177; size of, 39; skilled workers in, 71–75; trade deficit of, 6, 74–76; world export market, 78–80, 160
American Machinist, 21, 28, 63, 65, 93, 103, 126, 163
Android Corporation, 148–49
Armstrong, Arthur, 25
Army, United States, 29, 48, 59, 101, 103–6, 108–10
Ashburn, Anderson, 103
Asset Depreciation Range System, 142–44, 147
Automobile industry, 22–24, 26–31, 44, 60, 95, 105, 109–10, 112, 175; military demand in, 24, 30; R&D in, 48

B–1 Bomber, 58
Baldrige, Malcolm, 130

Bement, William, 19
Bendix Corporation, 118, 176
Bicycle industry, 20–22
Boeing, 103
Brock, William, 130
Brown, Harold, 148
Brown and Sharpe Manufactur-
  ing Company, 17–20, 42, 118;
  R&D of, 51
Bullard Company, 19–20
Business Week, 179

CAD/CAM (computer-aided de-
  sign and computer-aided man-
  ufacturing), 111
California, 44
Canada, 8, 131
Carlton Machine Tool Company,
  147–49
Carter administration, 58, 112,
  137
Census Bureau, 18, 42, 44
Center for Laser Studies, 59
Chrysler Corporation, 147–49
Cincinnati (Ohio), 22, 147
Cincinnati Milacron, Inc., 40, 42,
  102–3, 111, 118, 148, 177; R&D
  of, 50–51, 83 n.18
Civilian sector, problems in, 3–5,
  7, 56, 160
Civil War, 17–18, 173; machine
  tool demand from, 18
Cleveland (Ohio), 21–22,
  125–26
COCOM (Coordinating Commit-
  tee for Exports to Communist
  Countries), 131–32, 135, 138–
  41; members of, 131
Colt, 17
Communist countries, 8, 131–33,
  135–40. *See also* Eastern Bloc;
  Socialist countries
Consumption: of machine tools,

75, 76–77, 79, 88 n.74, 105,
  133, 135, 137, 139; by groups,
  93–95
Council of Economic Advisors,
  130, 160–61
Cross & Trecker, 42, 118; R&D
  in, 51
Czechoslovakia, 139

Danby Machine Corporation,
  149
Data Resources, Inc., 113
Defense (military) apparatus, 5,
  52, 95, 108, 139, 157, 159, 161,
  174. *See also* Defense (military)
  sector
Defense (military) contractors, 4,
  30, 58, 95–96, 104, 111–15, 122
  n.25. *See also* Prime military
  contractors
Defense (military) sector, 4–6, 8–
  9, 99, 161. *See also* Defense
  (military) apparatus
Defense spending (expenditures), 3, 7–8, 29, 61, 96, 101,
  104–6, 108–10, 158–63, 172,
  174, 180. *See also* Military
  spending (expenditures)
Department of Commerce, 89,
  119, 130, 132
Department of Defense, 59–60,
  85 n.38, 96, 98, 101, 104, 106,
  108–9, 111, 127, 132–33, 135,
  139–40, 148–49, 163; number of
  machine tools owned by, 95,
  126
Department of Energy, 133
Domestic International Sales
  Corporation, 142

Eastern Bloc, 133–35, 137–40; *See
  also* Communist Countries; Socialist countries

East Germany, 139
Economic hegemony (U.S.), threatened by foreign competition, 2
Economic Recovery Tax Act (ERTA), 144–45
Economics Ministry (West Germany), 52
Electrical discharge machining, 59
Electrochemical machining, 59
England (Great Britain), 14, 16, 18, 69, 76, 141
Export Administration Act: of 1969, 132–33, 135, 138, 141; of 1979, 141, 153 n.38; of 1983, 142
Export restrictions, resulting from defense policy, 8–9, 79, 132–33, 135, 140, 161
Exports (machine tool), stimulating demand, 19, 23, 28–29, 32, 34
Ex-Cell-O, 44, 118
Eximbank (Export-Import Bank), 136–37, 139
Exxon, 39

F–16 Fighter, 58
Faux, Jeff, 168–69
Federal military R&D, 2–3, 5–6, 51, 56, 60–61, 81–82, 158, 160, 168–69, 171; effects on productivity, 3; future growth of, 179; per capita, 54; as a percentage of GDP, 2, 54, 169; as a percentage of total federal R&D, 5, 55, 160; as a percentage of total R&D, 54, 160, 169
Finch, Stephen, 17
Flexible manufacturing systems (FMS), 85 n.38, 112
Ford Motor Company, 50–51

Foreign competition, 4, 8, 46, 52, 60, 69, 80, 110, 119–20, 131, 136, 158–59
Foreign governments, R&D support for industry, 8, 11 n.14, 52, 56, 76, 81–82, 115, 159, 161
Fortune, 39
France, 8, 135, 141
French machine tool producers (builders), 134–35, 137–38, 140

Geier, James, 40, 50
General Dynamics, 58, 103, 148
General Electric, 50, 58
General Motors, 39, 148–49, 172, 174–75, 177
Giddings & Lewis, Inc., 42, 57, 69, 119, 133
Gleason Works, 44; R&D in, 57
Government (U.S.), 2, 4, 6–7, 9, 14, 29, 31–32, 46, 61, 79, 112–13, 131, 136, 141–43, 147, 157–59, 161–62, 172, 174, 178–80; R&D spending for, 51, 62, 71, 81
Gray, James, 51, 66, 80
Greenwood and Batley, 18
Gridley, George, 25
Grumman, 103, 105

Hall, John, 15, 17
Harpers Ferry Armory, 15, 17
High energy rate forming machining, 59
High-speed machining, 59
Hot (laser) machining, 59
Houdaille Industries, Inc., 42, 129–30, 146

Illinois, 44
Indiana, 44
Industrial policy, 7, 75, 160–61, 171, 179–80
Inflation, 164–72, 174
Italian machine tool producers (builders), 134–35, 137–38, 140
Italy, 76, 135, 159
Interchangeable parts, 15–16
International Trade Commission, 63, 69, 115
Investment tax credit, 142–44, 147, 162–63

Jackson-Vanik Amendment, 133, 136–41, 153 n.32
Japan, 2, 7–8, 53–54, 56, 60–61, 69–70, 76, 79, 129, 131, 141, 143, 145, 159–60; per capita R&D, 54; productivity in, 65; spending on defense R&D, 2, 54–55, 169
Japan Development Bank, 53
Japanese machine tool builders (producers), 4, 7, 51–53, 61, 63, 69–72, 76, 79–82, 115, 117, 129–30, 134, 140, 143, 149, 159–60; R&D support for, 53, 161
Japanese machine tool industry, 7, 46, 72, 81, 115, 117, 143, 160–61; effects of defense spending on, 7, 115, 117, 120; types of companies in, 80–81; workers and wages in, 80–81; world export market, 78–81
Japan Machinery Exports Association, 129

Kearney & Trecker, 118, 177
Kennedy Round negotiations, 127–28

Keynesian policy, 1, 159, 168
Knudsen, William S., 29
Korean War, 2, 9, 32–34, 96–99, 109, 120

Lenin, Vladimir, 139
Litton Industries, 42
Lockheed Aircraft Corporation, 59, 103

McDonnell Douglas, 58, 103, 105
Machine tools: age of, 28, 31, 62–66, 102, 126, 161–64; arms production and, 14–21; computerized numerical control (CNC), 57–58, 102, 112; definition of, 13–14; direct numerical control (DNC), 57–58, 102, 112; domestic new orders of, 90–93, 95–97, 103–4, 107–9, 111, 113, 144–45, 164; early development of, 14–21; high prices of, 63–64, 67, 69, 79, 91, 144, 168, 171, 173; industrialization resulting form, 13; labor substituted for, 172–74; major users of, 93–95, 102; military contracts for, Parson 94–96, 104, 163; number of, 93, 112; numerical control (NC), 53, 56–58, 70–71, 102, 112, 141, 172
Machine tool companies (establishments): diversification of, 118–19; employment in, 31, 40, 42–43, 146; family control of, 40, 175; geographic location of, 44–45; investing abroad, 119; major ones, 42, 44; mergers, 118–19; number of, 41; sales and profits of, 45–48, 80; shipments of, 23, 25–28, 30–31, 42–43; size of, 40, 128

Machine Tool Laboratory of
   Aachen Technical University
   (West Germany), 53
McLean, Virginia, 125
Manufacturing Technology
   (Man-Tech) program, 85
   n.38
Marshall, George C., 30
Massachusetts Institute of Tech-
   nology (MIT), 57
Melman, Seymour, 5, 126
Merger movement, 21, 27
Michigan, 44
Middlefield (Connecticut), 17
Midwestern region, major pro-
   ducing area, 22, 26, 44
Military-industrial complex, 4–6,
   57, 102, 105
Military-Keynesian policy, 6–7,
   99, 112, 147
Military spending (expenditures),
   1–4, 7, 9. 33, 58, 82, 97, 103,
   104–6, 108–11, 120, 140, 157–
   61, 163, 169, 174; decreases of,
   6, 24–25, 31–33, 98–101, 104,
   109, 114–15, 122 n.28; future
   growth of, 179–80; increases
   of, 6–7, 23–24, 32, 96–101, 103–
   4, 112–14, 159, 164. See also
   Defense spending
   (expenditures)
Military spillovers and transference, 3, 10 n.5, 56–57, 160
Ministry of International Trade
   and Industry (MITI), 8, 54,
   129
Ministry of Research and Technology (West Germany), 52
Mitsubishi Corporation,
   147–49
Monarch Machine Tool Com-
   pany, 42

National Acme Manufacturing
   Company, 25–26
National Machine Tool Builders'
   Association, 8, 21–22, 30, 32,
   40, 46–47, 50–51, 56, 58, 66, 69,
   80, 97, 113, 125–33, 135–43,
   146–50. See also NMTBA
Navy, 29
New England, 16, 18–19,
   21–22
New Haven (Connecticut), 14
Nixon administration, 128
NMTBA. See National Machine
   Tool Builders' Association
Northrop, 103
North, Simeon, 15, 17

Office of Export Administration,
   141
Office of Management and
   Budget, 130
Ohio, 22, 44, 125

Parsons Corporation, 56–57
Peacekeeper missle, 180
Pentagon, 126–27, 149, 178, 180;
   cooperation with industry, 5–
   6, 52
Perkins, Tim, 69
Permanent war economy, 1, 3–7,
   97–99, 109, 159
Philadelphia, 19–22
Prime military contractors, 5, 95–
   96, 103, 106, 112, 148. See also
   Defense (military) contractors
Productivity (U.S.), 3–4, 62, 65,
   147, 164–74
Providence Tool Company, 17

Reagan administration, 112–13,
   129–30, 145, 149, 179
Recession(s), 91, 93, 98–99, 103,

107–11, 113–14, 129, 144–46,
  167, 173
Research Development Corpora-
  tion of Japan, 53
Rhode Island, 16–17
Robertson, Ross, 22
Rockwell International, 58,
  103
Rohr Industries, Inc., 177

Sellers, William, 19
Seromechanisms Laboratory,
  57
Slater, Samuel, 14
Socialist countries, 79, 133, 135,
  137–40. *See also* Eastern Bloc;
  Communist countries
Soviet Union (U.S.S.R.), 2, 135,
  137, 139
Spencer, Christopher, 17
Springfield (Massachusetts),
  17
Standard & Poors, 98
"Star Wars" technologies, 160
Stevenson, Adlai, 139
Stone, H. D., 17
Supply-side economics, 1, 7,
  112–13, 145–46, 162, 168, 178,
  181
Sweden, 132
Swiss machine tool producers
  (builders), 134–35, 140
Switzerland, 132

Taiwan, 76
Tax Equity and Fiscal Responsi-
  bility Act (TEFRA), 145
Technical Advisory Committee
  for Numerically Controlled
  Machine Tools, 141
Technical personnel, type of
  work, 2–3

Technological competency, in in-
  dustry, 6–7, 52, 56, 158–60
Technological lead, in machine
  tools, 7, 19, 23, 51–52, 56, 60–
  61, 84 n.22
Textron, Inc., 44
Tokyo, 130
Trade Act of 1974, 136
Trade balance (U.S.), 2–4
Trade Expansion Act of 1962,
  127–28, 130
Treasury Department, 128–29
Trident missle, 59, 180

Ultrasonic machining, 59
U.S. Arms Control and Disarma-
  ment Agency, 97, 108
U.S. Commodity Control List,
  139–40
United Technologies, 103
Urban Institute, 145

Vietnam War, 47, 66, 75, 93, 96–
  97, 114–15, 162–63, 169

War Industries Board, 24
Warner & Swasey, 118
Washington D.C., 125–27, 149
Watt, James, 14
West Germany, 7–8, 52–53, 60–
  61, 76, 79–80, 140, 143, 145,
  159; spending on defense
  R&D, 54–55, 169; per capita
  R&D, 54
West German machine tool
  builders (producers), 4, 7, 51–
  52, 61, 63, 69, 71–72, 76, 79–82,
  114, 117, 134–35, 138, 140, 143,
  149, 159–60; R&D support for,
  52–53
West German machine tool industry, 7, 46, 53, 72, 81, 114,
  137–38, 140, 143, 160; effects of

defense spending on, 7, 114–
15, 117, 120; types of companies, 80–81; workers and
wages in, 80–81; world export
market, 78–81
White Consolidated Industries,
42
Whitney, Eli, 14–17
Wilkinson, John, 14
Wisconsin, 44

World War I, 22, 26, 31; effect on
machine tool demand, 23–26,
33, 96; female workers in machine tool firms, 24
World War II, 2, 4–5, 9, 46, 57,
61, 115, 157–58, 161; effect on
machine tool demand, 27–34,
96, 98

XM–1 tanks, 147–49

About the Author

ANTHONY DIFILIPPO is Assistant Professor of Sociology at Lincoln University in Pennsylvania. He has contributed to *Social Science Review*.